Counter-Terrorism and Human Rights

Counter-Terrorism and Human Rights

David J. Whittaker

Longman
is an imprint of

Harlow, England • London • New York • Boston • San Francisco • Toronto • Sydney • Singapore • Hong Kong
Tokyo • Seoul • Taipei • New Delhi • Cape Town • Madrid • Mexico City • Amsterdam • Munich • Paris • Milan

PEARSON EDUCATION LIMITED

Edinburgh Gate
Harlow CM20 2JE
United Kingdom
Tel: +44 (0)1279 623623
Fax: +44 (0)1279 431059
Website: www.pearsoned.co.uk

First edition published in Great Britain in 2009

ISBN: 978-1-4058-9980-2

British Library Cataloguing in Publication Data
A CIP catalogue record for this book can be obtained from the British Library

Library of Congress Cataloging in Publication Data
Whittaker, David J., 1925–
    Counter-terrorism and human rights / David J. Whittaker.
        p. cm.
    Includes bibliographical references and index.
    ISBN 978-1-4058-9980-2 (pbk. : alk. paper)   1. Terrorism – United States –
Prevention.   2. Terrorism – Great Britain – Prevention.   3. Terrorism –
European Union countries – Prevention.   4. Human rights.   I. Title.
K5256.W48 2009
363.325′16—dc22

                                                                    2009022551

10   9   8   7   6   5   4   3   2   1
13   12   11   10   09

Set 9/14pt Stone Serif by 35
Printed in Great Britain by Henry Ling Ltd, Dorchester, Dorset

The Publisher's policy is to use paper manufactured from sustainable forests.

Contents

Acknowledgements

I am indebted to a number of people for their time and patience and invaluable advice in the making up of this book:

Mari Shullaw, Christina Wipf-Parry and Jessica Harrison at Pearson Education; Joanna Stephenson at the Royal Commonwealth Society;

Bill Joseph and Adrian Norton for ironing out technical difficulties;

Skeeby Computer Services for typing service;

Marianne Whittaker for painstaking reading of the manuscript in draft and most helpful criticism.

Publisher's acknowledgements

We are grateful to the following for permission to reproduce copyright material:

Extract on page 35 from Whittaker, D., *Terrorism: Understanding the Global Threat* (Pearson Education, 2006), courtesy of Pearson Education Ltd; extract on page 51 from Letters page, *The Guardian*, 24/12/2007 (McNulty, Tony), copyright Guardian News & Media Ltd 2007; extract on page 70 from *The Guardian* (courtesy of Gearty, C).

In some instances we have been unable to trace the owners of copyright material, and we would appreciate any information that would enable us to do so.

Introduction

A companion volume to this book had the title *Terrorism: Understanding the Global Threat*. It has seemed necessary in a twin volume to go much further and look carefully at what we can do to deal with this threat. Issues to do with counter-terrorism policies are growing ever more significant internationally. Once again, readers can be sure of one thing, namely, that what appears here in print is not all to be understood as the last word. In this case we have a scrutiny of present-day thinking about counter-terrorism and action together with a preliminary discussion of possible lines in the future. Facts and discussion will move from 'what is' to 'what might or ought to be'. Put plainly, the overall purpose is to inform, to speculate a little and, most certainly, to encourage further enquiry and debate. Polemics will be left to the user of the book.

Terror, terrorism and terrorists are words heard every day, everywhere. What they lack, though, whether in print or in spoken usage is agreed, standard meaning. These terms are set in contexts that are generally disputable, vague, and contradictory. Prejudgement, generalisation, even prejudice seem inescapable. Terror has always been a personal reaction in the sense that William Shakespeare used it in *Richard III* – 'so full of dismal terror was the time!' In more modern years terror is commonly viewed as a planned artifice by malevolent individuals or groups. Terrorism demands urgent, collective action to counter it and to restore secure normality. Countering it, though, risks our loss of freedom and elemental human rights. Protection, yes, but at what price?

In the United Kingdom Parliament is continually being asked to approve more and more surveillance procedures which even the retiring Director of Public Prosecution, Sir Ken MacDonald, has considered as 'powers that would break freedom's back'. His 'relentless prosecutional struggle against terrorism' (with conviction rate in excess of 90 per cent) has been conducted, he believes, with restraint and with public and individual rights kept prominently in mind.

Terrorism is wide, deep and unpredictable. This introduction is being written during a week, in October 2008, when some terrorist activity returns both to Northern Ireland and South Africa, where, after longed-for quiet, there has been a reintroduction of gunshots, the raw edge of sectarian infighting. The fragility of reconciliation after terror will certainly underlie facts and hopes in many of the following chapters.

This book will attempt to clarify and disentangle some of the main counter-terrorism problems, such as that of finding a balance between operating strategies and programmes and the importance of conserving human rights. A first chapter presents key issues. Although these issues crop up later, examined in detail, it is considered useful to outline them as 'headers' at the outset. Subsequent chapters range over basic human rights, counter-terrorism in law and practice, the controversies surrounding detention, preliminary charging and court work, punishment and rendition. The approach had to be selective in dealing with issues of the United States, the United Kingdom, Europe and South-east Asia. As far as possible, questions are addressed objectively without attention to conspiracy theories. A section 'Where to find out more' will be found on pages 190–92.

In conclusion, something ex-President Clinton said in 2004 at an American Legion dinner is worth repeating. He said of counter-terrorism that an important priority would be to dismantle the 'boxes', in which most of us live, to break down barriers and to mix more freely and tolerantly with others. Terrorism, so he believes, is often the last desperate pitch of the humiliated and the hungry with so many of their rights denied. 'It is the raw message of those who are neither heard nor understood. Effective counter-terrorism programmes benefit from recruiting not only doers but listeners.'

chapter

Key issues

C ounter-terrorism has to do with the prevention and control of terrorism. Assertions such as this immediately raise
pressing demands and beg almost countless questions.
Popular outrage and calls for retaliation are an understandable
reaction to tragic and indiscriminate incidents and killings but
the response of a state must be rational and proportionate.
Implementation of protective programmes to offset terrorism
puts into focus an array of critical issues to do with maintenance
of security and the assurance of fundamental human rights.
Many of the ethical issues raised in regard to freedom of person,
speech, association and movement arouse widespread anxiety,
controversy, protest and some anger, if they appear compromised or reduced. Should there be limits to our right to protest,
especially where it is held to involve 'indirect action' or an
'incitement' to others to act? Protest soon begins to focus on the
state's resort to surveillance, arrest, criminal charge, detention
and deportation. Is it basically humane, it is asked, to treat suspect in the ruthless fashion we commonly employ? Can it be
right to label some people as suspects when there is so little to
justify premature action? What safeguards prevent misjudgements and hasty, inappropriate procedures?

Governments in many parts of the world are increasingly devising
and employing protective strategies against terrorism, something

they regard rather as a tidal force. There are now clear, vociferous calls in many lands for tighter controls where rights may be downgraded against principles of enhanced collective security. Liberal-minded people and lawyers everywhere are unhappy about many prescriptive measures, their purpose and tactical application. States wrestle more and more with uncertainties and contradictions. The now outmoded talk of a War on Terror referred to a world needing to brace itself in the face of a pandemic. More careful thinking reveals violence as a consequence of extreme political radicalism and, further, as diverse, complex, shifting in motivation, nature, direction and extent. Seen in this way it appears most unlikely that terrorist activities, whether destructive disablement of society or heroic 'freedom fighting', can be countered by states acting independently in piecemeal fashion according to a morass of mainly self-interested principles. The Big Fight notion of 'total-action-defeats-total-terror' has a beguiling simplicity and an unproductive dividend. We must do better than that to tackle the specific nature of violence and to make sure that it is done with absolute regard for the preservation of human rights.

Chapter 2 takes a good look at basic human rights agreed at the United Nations (UN) – the Universal Declaration of Human Rights (1948), the International Covenant on Civil and Political Rights (1966) and the International Covenant on Economic, Social and Political Rights (1987). Additionally there is the European Convention on Human Rights, ratified in 1953. Those who consult these documents will be able to gauge for themselves how far a number of assured democratic values and standards are challenged by many counter-terrorism operational policies and legislation. Binding articles in instruments such as that of the International Criminal Court, the United Nations Declaration on the Rights of Indigenous People and the Council of Europe Convention on Terrorism lay down obligations in the light of which we may judge how far these are honoured or denied by state governments, non-governmental organisations (NGOs) and politicians when the need to preserve internal stability and security is intoned. Old dilemmas stand plain. How can citizens of a sovereign state be protected against rights violations even by their own states? Are political leaders deterred from resorting to isolating themselves if they realise that one day they may be prosecuted under international law? These days, covenant texts are unlikely to be read in comfort. Cynics and pessimists crowd in alongside optimists. Many will hold judgements or censure states for hypocrisy and disregard of elemental human principles where priority is given more often to narrow, political considerations.

Countering terrorism needs policy articulated, strengthened and enforced through legislation. Once again, states and concerned individuals come up against problems of definition, clarity and appropriateness. Are the lawmakers sufficiently knowledgeable about political factors that ultimately encourage protest, dissatisfaction, demonstration and violence?

Even a preliminary survey of legislation approved and enacted in numerous countries does not show too much consistency nor close attention to significant detail in regard to how 'suspects' are categorised, charged and sent for trial. Quite the greatest difficulty is in bringing into balance and mutual application the law systems and provisions of a number of countries working in collaboration against terrorism. Security agencies here and there appear to pay scant attention to legal criteria. In a context of crisis, legislators will be required to stand aside 'from the job being done'. Lives have to be saved, it is said, even if some of our liberties and legalities have to be sidestepped or sacrificed altogether.

Following terrorist incidents, there is often a swelling approval of tough lines of action by responsible authority. A strategy planned by a state to expedite counter-terrorism is approved, if not always applauded at the outset. Tactics incorporating surveillance (direct and indirect), disputed detention, arrest, the vagaries of charging procedure, premature extradition, the transfer and transport of suspects, their treatment on interrogation and the imprisonment of those not too carefully indicted, all eventually lead to widespread questioning, fierce controversy, even anger at the loss for human rights. In so many instances, a state's stratagem of 'bringing terrorists to justice as swiftly as possible' needs reappraisal of the fundamental issues at stake by the liberal-minded.

As we shall see in later chapters, it is in the area of government strategies to counter-terrorism that the Big Issues of a state's responsibilities and citizens' human rights meet and frequently collide. Two interesting examples of State versus People seen in the United States and in the United Kingdom are discussed in Chapter 4. This chapter will outline a number of salient issues and undoubtedly these will be met with again subsequently.

From the steps of the White House federal responsibility for Protecting America has frequently received presidential emphasis. On 6 March 2008 President George W. Bush described a strategy against terrorism that would prevent and disrupt attack, protect the people, apply a comprehensive approach to risk management and put into place measures to respond to any incident and recover from it. Altogether, state and people were to share a Culture of Preparedness.

What a splendid statement of readiness as seen on Capitol Hill! This affirmation, though, and some of those in previous years have been criticised widely, particularly by the American Civil Liberties Union (ACLU). They have had much to say about US anti-terrorism legislation. Issues raised in the injunction to Make America Safe have drawn much liberal fire. Citizens are told that the state's preparedness will enable them to Live Safely. Way back in June 2006 the ACLU put the matter of safe existence quite sternly:

The US Government has seriously eroded the right to privacy by expanding its surveillance of ordinary Americans in the name of protecting national security. The NSA (National Security Agency) is conducting massive wiretapping and data mining of phone calls and emails and the FBI (Federal Bureau of Investigation) is spying upon peaceful political and religious groups and demanding personal records without court approval or probably cause. Dissent is now treated as unpatriotic.

> In the view of ACLU the state in its 'preparedness' should at least prohibit absolutely any 'indefinite', mandatory detention of individuals who pose no security risk. The rights of the criminally accused must be respected. Domestic surveillance erodes the right to privacy and must be ended. Children's rights are to be guaranteed. Freedom of thought, conscience and religion must be ensured. The obligation to allow free expression and peaceful assembly is to be honoured.

> Again, in June 2006, the ACLU was detecting 'disturbing trends' in the Administration's resolve to build Security and Safety:

Threats (that) undermine the rule of law in America, the assumption that the Executive has unchecked authority to ignore law. To regain our position as a beacon of freedom throughout the world the US must protect the fundamental freedoms and rights enshrined in the U.S. Constitution.

> It would seem that Living Safely for the Americans has everything to do with Living Assuredly in the assurance that human rights are pre-eminently acknowledged and secured. The ACLU, with 500,000 members, is itself in danger of being placed on a Washington 'black list'. Nevertheless, there is ongoing attention being paid to the primacy of human rights despite campaigning difficulties. A recent instance of this is ACLU's determined effort to put an end to 'warrantless surveillance'. This investigative tactic was found unconstitutional by a federal district court in Michigan at the end of 2007. An end to it was ordered since it violated the Fourth Amendment of the Constitution. Washington appealed. In March 2008 the appeal was lost and

the Government went back to its wiretapping and invasion of privacy.

Debate over key issues faces difficulties inherent in a vocabulary that features such concepts as 'acts preparatory to terrorism', 'suspected behavior and intent', 'terrorist militancy' and the 'proscription' of suspected groups. Definition seen from the perspective of the security controller is frequently couched simplistically. Who is to decide to what degree 'extremism' and 'unacceptable behaviour' are rated criminal? Critics, particularly in the United Kingdom and the United States, worry about targeting and community alienation when the police make a first approach or level a control order.

Finally, we have a stark issue facing both politician and lawyer. How temporary is temporary? How permanent is an edict, a proscriptive measure and an exclusion order? For how long can basic human rights be suspended while a security operation is in progress? In another field, for example, is it credible that the United States can blackball an Iranian organisation, the People's Mujahedin of Iran (PMOI) for virtually a decade when political circumstances appear to have changed markedly? Originally viewed as militant and violent, PMOI is now taken to be a legitimate opposition front, working for democratic engagement with other countries. By all accounts they have given up weaponry, preferring the easy accessibility and careful messages of the Internet. More realistically, in the summer of 2008, Washington removed North Korea from the list of terrorism 'sponsors'. Very clearly, issues in debate have to take account of political factors changing in style, direction and emphasis.

Meanwhile, in the United Kingdom, key issues to do with human rights are rarely absent from the media. Debate over the government proposal to extend detention to 48 days has been fierce and, as we shall see later, undoubtedly influenced the House of Lords on 14 October 2008 to reject the provision. A day later,

Lord Carlile, the Government's own reviewer of anti-terrorism laws, described a projected, huge database of personal data as a 'raw idea' and 'awful'; and as something calling for tight controls in usage.

There might be a slight element of reassurance that key issues of personal freedom and privacy are not to be cast aside by Whitehall when both Lord Carlile and Lord West, Home Office minister and military intelligence chief, warn us in the same October week about any reliance on a 'Big Brother' type of society. Indeed, as Liberty had put it on 11 June 2008, 'recent events have shown how Britain's moral compass has left our country less safe . . .'

Human rights in principle

I f democracies are to counter terrorism successfully can this be done without endangering, possibly sacrificing, basic liberties, laws and fundamental human rights? This is a critical question discussed in this chapter. First, the main principles of human rights agreed internationally will be outlined. Second, there is some account of what might be termed monitoring institutions set up by human rights bodies. Chapter 3 surveys the 'state of play', namely, the extent of observance or neglect of fundamental human rights around the world, especially as this relates to counter-terrorist policies. Principles and their consequences are detailed and complex. (Readers, however, will be able to examine these for themselves by using Internet keywords and websites.)

UN principles

Concepts and values of human rights, especially in Europe, have been put about since Ancient Greece and, above all, during the eighteenth-century Age of Enlightenment. Today most trace the detailed study and public exposition of these rights to the coming together of nations in the UN as the Second World War ended in 1945. Mindful of a barbarous conflict there was a great interest in devising charters, covenants and conventions to reaffirm (as the UN Charter expressed it) 'faith in fundamental human rights and in the dignity and worth of the human person'.

It was an American president's wife, Eleanor Roosevelt, who, in 1948, vigorously steered a committee, the UN Commission of Human Rights, in the design of a set of human rights principles for submission to the UN's General Assembly. Two and a half years of intensive work went into the framing of a bill. For this determined champion, it was said, the hopes of H. W. Longfellow became her daily invocation:

Sail on, O Union, strong and great. Humanity with all its fears, with all the hopes of future years, is hanging breathless on thy fate.

The principles in the bill would not be the product of any particular ethical tradition; rather, they represented the lowest common denominator of human values understood as a reaction to the horrors of the Second World War. In taking up aspirations, declaring goals and establishing moral norms the bill would blaze a trail condemning violation and offering protection.

There would be three parts to the measure: a Universal Declaration, supporting Covenants and an Optional Protocol. The General Assembly adopted the Universal Declaration on 10 December 1948 by 48 votes to nil with 8 abstentions (the Soviet bloc countries, apartheid South Africa and Saudi Arabia).

Thirty articles in the Universal Declaration attest that all men are born free and equal in dignity and rights and that they are entitled to rights and freedoms without any distinction. A long list of political, economic, cultural and social rights is set out. Among rights enumerated are that all human beings are born free and equal in dignity and rights – a re-echo of the famous assertion in the US Constitution. Highly relevant today in the context of countering terrorism are the essential rights to freedom from arbitrary arrest, detention or exile, and freedom from inhuman, cruel and degrading treatment or punishment. Individual privacy must never be subject to arbitrary interference.

Essentially, an individual must be presumed innocent until guilt is proven – a long established principle in English common law, as are the rights to freedom of thought, conscience and religion and of peaceful association and assembly. It is an impressive list, but there are several points worth remembering. In the first place, entitlement cannot be guaranteed. In many circumstances it will be advisable for an individual or some sort of pressure group to press for observance and necessary action. Rights can be laid down but they are associated with duties which no individual is to ignore and this will be a matter for conscience and fellow feeling. A stipulation much debated forbids interference in matters that are 'essentially within the jurisdiction of any state'. This is a difficult question-begging statement. Could it not provide an escape clause for rogue governments? Certainly, as concerns internal security many states fall back on what they regard as permitted autonomy. At a time of terrorist threat to ordered life, a resort to what would normally be branded as unwarranted repression is often justified in the light of 'needs must . . .'.

For most observers the Universal Declaration might be thought to bring about a transformation from the horizontal plane (where rights are conferred by states within a comity of nations) to the vertical plane (where rights reach down to individual men and women). Where the UN Charter of 1945 is largely states-centric, the Declaration and other documents distinguish moral and inalienable rights as the legitimate expectations of the common man. It is encouraging to see how many of these moral values have been incorporated into the customary law of nations, including new states emerging from old empires.

The framing of covenants

Listing the principles of human rights was perhaps the easiest task for the UN in the process of legislation. What had to be done next was to frame covenants that bound the signatories. The conversion of Declaration principles into treaties and the elaboration of procedures for their implementation was to take ten years of preparation; they finally came into force in 1976. Two covenants were designed; an International Covenant on Civil and Political Rights and an International Covenant on Economic, Social and Cultural Rights. Ready adoption of these measures was only likely if they were kept separate from each other . . . Indeed, 40 years later prevarication over some articles in these covenants can be met with in many lands.

The International Covenant on Civil and Political Rights (1966), the covenant of most concern to this chapter, is chiefly a prescriptive measure in that 160 ratifying states are obliged to report on their implementation through legislation and everyday practice to a UN Human Rights Committee. They have to stand up and be counted so that their policies are visible to the rest of the world . . . Exposure of a violation or neglect of human rights will not often lead to admission of neglect and then compliance but, as in the instances of torture practice, summary court practice or forced 'disappearances', there will be international publicity and censure. Sanctions have generally brought about a policy change on the part of recalcitrant regimes. Fifty-three articles spell out in great detail what is required of signatory states.

The Covenant guarantees to everyone the right to life itself and to self-determination without distinction of any kind. Should there be reasons why an individual is apprehended or extradited, these reasons must be made plain, detention must give way to prompt charging, all accusations of criminality have to be substantiated and there is to be no leaning back on blanket treatment of possible 'suspects'. Clearly, at the moment, many states, including the United Kingdom and the United States, are obviously contravening the letter and spirit of the Covenant in regard to summary arrest, detention without charge, the vagaries of named charges, the obtaining and compilation of evidence and the reliance on secretive investigations and interviewing of a suspect's associates. As is well known, security authorities in London and Washington plead the case of extreme terrorist threat to the need to derogate from basic principles. Apart from this element of derogation there is the standing aside of certain Islamic states – Sudan, Pakistan, Iran, Saudi Arabia and Kuwait, who see the Universal Declaration and the Covenants as not taking account of Islam's cultural and religious contexts.

Is the Covenant not expressly designed to help the individual rather than the state? This is the purpose of the subsidiary Optional Protocol, a measure to assist those who feel victimised by a state's faulty observance of fundamental rights. Human rights treaties are usefully followed by an optional protocol which provides for procedures with regard to the treaty. A state which has ratified the Protocol is enabled to conduct enquiries into individual or widespread complaints about treaty violation or evasion . . . Complaints are to be sent in writing to the UN Human Rights Committee. The state complained against must have ratified both the International Covenant on Civil and Political Rights and the Optional Protocol. The Protocol can include more detail about matters included in the treaty and there is scope for dealing with issues that have come up since the treaty was written. It is possible that the Protocol can propose rights and obligations that were not in the original treaty. A number of quite significant complaints have been forwarded to the Human Rights Committee recently. Complaints have been sent in as to the rights of women in Dubai and Saudi Arabia, election irregularities in Chile, forced-labour routines in Turkey and the use of torture in counter-terrorism interviewing . . . In June 2008 a group of Islamic imams in London were prepared to take advantage of the Protocol . . . They were incensed by government readiness to forbid what was seen as inflammatory preaching in the mosque. Do we not have some freedom of speech, the imams ask? Are we really likely to encourage would-be terrorists when we discharge our religious obligations to the faithful?

It is interesting to consider for a moment what happens when signatory states meet to discuss human rights and counter-terrorism arrangements. In matters which are thought to compromise jealously guarded sovereignty, discussion sometimes takes the form of turning a disapproving spotlight on the reputed machinations of others. This self-righteous pose in the political cockpit can usefully divert the critics. Hopefully, really thorny problems, such as identifying the intentions of terrorist suspects, detention policies and rendition, can be worked on positively and quietly in small meeting rooms.

The business of securing international accord among governments is not all made easier by Article 2.7 of the UN Charter which prohibits signatories interfering 'in matters essentially within the jurisdiction of member states' . . . There is an element of irony here with a clause which could be viewed as quite opposed to the concept of international decision-in-accord. At least, in recent years, many world leaders have counselled their governments to think carefully about the disadvantages of a Keep Out preference and the possibilities of consensual intervention in cases of flagrant inhumane violation.

European human rights principles

Europe, too, has its own Human Rights Convention with principles modelled on those of the UN. It is worth taking a brief look at them. The Convention for the Protection of Human Rights and Fundamental Freedoms, also known as the European Convention on Human Rights, was adopted under the auspices of the Council of Europe as long ago as 1950, though final ratifications took another three years. After all, in accepting the Convention 21 autonomous nations were thereby agreeing to submit certain human rights controversies to the binding determination of an international body. Equally novel, in a sense, was that the majority of signatories approved an optional provision granting individuals and private associations the right to file a complaint. As we have noted earlier these requirements were not easy to square with traditional notions of independence in judgements and action.

The Convention consists of numerous articles embodying fundamental principles. Explicitly Europe's citizens have inviolable rights to life, liberty, security and a fair trial and freedom from torture and 'inhuman and degrading treatment or punishment'. There is to be a freedom of thought, conscience, religion, expression, assembly and association. A series of protocols binds European states to uphold these principles. In many respects the Europeans were keen to put more definiteness into their Convention. States' commitments would bind them to observance more strongly and there was to be a watchfulness through investigation and report against veering away from loyalty to agreed principles. Undeniably, progress in building machinery to defend rights has been slow beyond the declaration stage. One material achievement, though, among neighbourly nations is today's general recognition that no government protecting individual and group rights can pretend to enjoy the absolute, reserved jurisdiction into which international law is unable to penetrate.

The Convention, not 50 yeas old, is regarded by the European Court of Human Rights as a 'living instrument'. This means that as society, attitudes and challenges change so the Court will change and develop ways in which it interprets the Convention. Since the turn of the century, undoubtedly with security concerns in mind, the United Kingdom has decided to make certain convention rights clearer to British citizens and to incorporate these rights in the Human Rights Act 1998, made law in 2000. Now certain rights are to be made plain for implementation by government and by all public authorities who are to monitor their own compliance with the Act's requirements.

Rights significant in the context of security alerts and counterterrorism are as follows:

Absolute rights – uninfringeable, e.g. the right to prohibition of torture and degrading treatment;

Qualified rights – the state may lawfully interfere in certain circumstances, e.g. the right to respect for private life and family;

Limited rights – circumstances may restrict or abbreviate rights, e.g. the right to liberty and security.

This comprehensive Human Rights Act lays out rights of suspects, of peaceful protest, of prisoners, of defendants, of freedom of thought, conscience and religion, of not being discriminated against, of no punishment without law and of freedom of association and assembly.

At this point, one must suppose that the sheer breadth of the Act's provisions, together with the debatable nature of *qualified* and *limited* rights, has occasioned innumerable contests of opinion, legal and lay, since 2000. Unavoidably, the atmosphere today is charged with terrorist incidents, actual and hypothetical threats and a restrictive attitude towards those categorised as 'suspects'. Certain counter-terrorism measures when enforced seem incompatible with one or two rights proclaimed by the Act. Altogether the United Kingdom's Human Rights Act 2000 is regarded by most people as helpful and a blessing, perhaps a mixed one.

There is little doubt that most people feel sad at the mismatch between plain, ethical consensus and the reality of what happens on the ground. As we shall see in a later section of this chapter, there is an array of what might be termed monitoring bodies empowered to watch for movement away from what has been declared right and proper.

Interestingly, Europe's effort to set down human rights principles has brought commendation from more than one US commentator. What circumstances enable the Europeans to draft such a list of rights successfully? Well, primarily, their Convention was limited to traditional civil and political rights already guaranteed widely in the countries of Western Europe. Then, the legal systems of the Member States were appreciably homogeneous and helpful in aiding interpretation and application of the provisions. Certainly, a preference for settling issues through painstaking negotiation rather than through any brainstorming public forum was a great advantage. There were, of course, language difficulties but this did not prevent careful screening of any complaint or petition. In many respects these special, advantageous conditions were unlikely to be easily replicated elsewhere and particularly in the United States (a place remarkable both for union and disunion).

The United States and human rights

The American continent also has human rights principles detailed in documents signed by participants. In 1959 the Inter-American Commission on Human Rights (IACHR) was set up. A permanent body meeting regularly in Washington, the Commission was given the task of promoting observance of fundamental principles already in print in the Organization of American States (OAS) Charter, the American Declaration of the Rights and Duties of Man and the American Convention on Human Rights. All this was very much in line with the spirit of UN declaratory work and, indeed, its canvas was a broader one than the ones drafted and signed in the UN and in the European Convention. One innovation, possibly reflecting vibrant US democracy, was that a number of important human rights were defined, mainly at the urging of NGOs, not as individual rights as such but as collective rights, that is, in relation to the self-determination rights of groups or of ethnic minorities. A great deal of effort goes into campaigns and activities to arouse public awareness. The Americans are also keen to reckon with the very sensitive inter-relationships between political and judicial factors, things that have slowed down unanimity among diverse European national systems. In the New World, 35 nations, members of OAS, are enjoined to take to heart a very demanding agenda. As we shall see later in this chapter the monitoring of such a complex remit is thorough and large in scale. As in Europe, however, the very extent of principled enumeration and description convinces some people that there are too many flourishes, here and there too much vagueness and opportunities for ambiguity, all providing loopholes for the unprincipled in government office.

Africa and human rights

Africa has seen a longstanding attempt to delineate and promote fundamental rights in a continent noted for their flagrant disregard. It was fairly recently, in the 1980s, that there met together a group of African nations profoundly disturbed by the continent's instabilities. In addition to civil war and ethnic rivalry, Africa on all sides was seen as hugely inhuman and discriminating in its multiple internal relationships. That and the constant recourse in modern times to violence with car bombs and incendiarism called urgently for collective thinking and positive experiment. The other two continents to west and east had followed the example of the UN in committing themselves and everybody else to legislation to advance human rights. Leading Africans thought they should do something similar.

The Africa Charter on Human and People's Rights, known also as the Banjul Charter, was most carefully drawn up and drafted to suit the preferences of a committed group of thinkers. Somehow it had to declare principles that a very varied audience, varied in ethnic origin, in language and in religion, might ultimately acknowledge and appreciate. The very title of the document incorporating people's rights was a ploy to eradicate all traces of colonialism, that historical legacy new, developing nations were determined to forget. Articles in the UN Declaration and

Covenants serve as inspiring examples of what should be secured: most certainly the rights to individual, unrestricted freedom, to equality, to justice and to dignity would be splendid to intone, given the uncertainties and difficulties many African communities face. In a most explicit way rights must be declared as inalienable, indivisible and interconnected, stressing emphatically the relationship of rights and responsibilities. Was this not a tremendous challenge to put to people so recently emerging from colonial dependence, if not subjugation? In how many years had Africans had a chance to exercise any degree of freedom? Put plainly what was the likelihood of a popular, intelligible and willing response from a population only recently enfranchised and schooled (in the widest sense)? Further, and deserving an answer, how far would a set of abstract principles appeal to hungry people menaced by terror in various shapes? Six years of summit discussion went into the process of ratification and the Charter arrived in 1986. Two initiatives along the way enabled clarification and decision. Two advisory bodies were bought into being: the Africa Commission and the Africa Human Rights Research Center. The latter struck up links with universities in Denmark and Sweden to collaborate on problems of rights interpretation, promotion and public education. Most useful were discussions about handling violations, either obvious in the field or filed in complaints and petitions. Africa, the last to enter the charter scene, was not slow in learning.

South-east Asia and human rights

A group of South-east Asian nations has lost little time in emulating the rights promotion of northern continents. In so many respects Asians live in a community harassed by virulent interethnic rivalry and strife and the ready use of explosives. Already in 1995 initial consultations as to a possible Human Rights Charter were taking place in numerous capitals in the region among government ministers, and leaders of provincial authorities and minorities. Annual summits were to do the spadework. By November 2007 the ink was dry and 10 South-east Asian flags flew over Singapore as a charter was signed. Signatories were Brunei, Burma (Myanmar), Cambodia, Indonesia, Laos, Malaysia, the Philippines, Singapore, Thailand and Vietnam.

Political issues intruded upon delegates' discussion until almost the last moment. Terrorist outrage appeared endemic in the region. Nations then had to be tough about internal liberties if they were to survive. More worryingly Burma's appalling military dictatorship made their charter participation most questionable. Might that fact invite outside interference, something the members could not contemplate? Cambodia, Laos and Vietnam had authoritarian, heavy-handed regimes. The rights records and security provisions in the Philippines raised tough issues. And elsewhere in Asia there would be much to do to bring the Koreans and Japanese into line with rights tolerance if membership were to expand. Nobody can yet exclude the hobbling of progress with the Charter if its translation into reality becomes entwined in political infighting, national vetoes and over-zealous police work. Everyone is concerned, of course, at the likelihood of tighter security crackdowns in the battle against terrorism.

The monitoring of rights principles

An impressive array of fundamental human rights principles has been presented by the UN and by bodies meeting together in several continents. What, though, are the means by which these bodies attempt to secure full observance of principles now confirmed by international accord? We can expect there to be arrangements for the monitoring of complete and final observance through regular survey, investigation and report. From time to time the nature of states' implementation may be a matter for comment and discussion given the importance of various political factors. Quite clearly, the work of monitoring agencies (if that term may be used) will be ongoing, complex and necessarily firm in intent.

The UN's statement of principles is watched over by three institutions – the Commission on Human Rights, the Human Rights Council and the International Court of Justice.

The Commission on Human Rights

This Commission was instituted in 1946 when the UN felt sure that amity and close agreement would prevail as to the essentials of civilised living. A panel of experts would deal with any matter relating to human rights through enquiry, periodic report and recommendations for action. Anything less than unswerving acknowledgement of the rights agenda could be treated through good-tempered negotiation and even modification of some points. Sub-commissions were to appoint rapporteurs or working groups to deal with special topics and with any indication of a nation's disloyalty to international consensus. This was novel in two respects. First, instances of gross rights of violation could be pounced upon, studied and revealed to all Member States inviting firm condemnation and restorative action. Second, it was now made possible for an individual to file a complaint with the UN for violation of rights. Previously, it had been almost unthinkable that a citizen could complain to an international body against their own government. Redress against eviction, torture, summary arrest or injury might now be achieved. Bona fide grievances would be spotlighted and dealt with promptly.

Unhappily, the fine hopes of the Commission's formative years were not to last. Irritated partisanship soured conciliation. Minority rights, in particular, were denied, even savaged, in Syria, Indonesia, Iran, Iraq, Turkey, Russia, Colombia and Ecuador. Within 10 years or so these states were being pilloried under scrutiny for their alleged rights violations. Claim, counter-claim and vituperative anecdotes were so common in the Commission's

Geneva office that one member declared 'it was a wonderful place to disagree in'. Something stronger than the Commission was needed.

In several respects a successor to the weakened Commission must have 'bite' as well as 'bark'. There must be authority to take rights offenders by the collar and to insist on restorative action. There must be authority to cope with recalcitrant members' resort to loopholes, ambiguities and dishonesty. There must be a means of straightening out those governments who could never accept being 'named and shamed'. Out in the confused, fearful world was it not absolutely vital to deter governments from limiting rights when that had been considered necessary by 'the exigencies of a situation'? Otherwise, the imperatives of a counter-terrorism programme, say, would gravely imperil rights and liberties. Yet, the UN still has no way of forcing governments to change their policies or practice. Persuasion is the only tool that may be used to work for improvements in regard to human rights. All UN procedures have to aim at focusing the persuasive weight of international opinion against a wrongdoer.

The Human Rights Council

The Commission gave way on 15 March 2006 to a new Human Rights Council with 190 nations hoping that a political mire could be satisfactorily drained. It was urgent to meet the criticism of the former Commission (often voiced by the United States) that some members acquired high-status profile though they were failing to guarantee the fundamental rights of their own people. No longer would a member be allowed to use the human rights forum to deflect criticism of a shoddy human rights record. A state applying for membership of the Council would need the approval of a majority of members. The ballot would be secret. Furthermore, should a member be convicted of rights violation then they would be suspended.

Council membership varies from year to year. Two terms' membership is the rule. In 2008 there are 47 states as members: 13 from Africa, 13 from Asia, 8 from Latin America, 6 from Eastern Europe, 7 from a rather quaintly termed Western Europe and Others which provides for a far-off Canada. Neither the United States nor Israel were prepared to join the Council in 2006 for reasons we shall consider shortly. The Council was to meet more regularly than the unwieldy Commission.

Something of a fanfare greeted the Council's inception in Geneva. At last a new body was to bring decisiveness, a fair measure of objectivity and constructive concern to the implementation of humanity's human rights. An aspect of the new resolve exciting many was that the UN's institution was setting out to collaborate with 'stakeholders' representing NGOs, advisory groups, think tanks of many persuasions and various lands. A reconstituted and revitalised body would be much more suited to the task of lacing together measures to square up to the universal threat of terrorism. Several controlling and enhancing mechanisms would be set up – termed Special Procedures, Special Sessions and Universal Periodic Review.

Special Procedures were to be the remit of an elect group of experts reporting back to Geneva instances of human rights violations, country by country. Determination and furrowed brows would yield opinion on specific complaints and incidents. The group would be in a position to conduct studies of discriminatory practice and to furnish advice as to how to secure proper observance. One of these advisory parties, the Working Group on Terrorism is currently examining very deliberately case studies of terrorist activities and counter-terrorism, especially the legal and operational aspects. However, this reliance on observers' full knowledge and objectivity is meeting with some doubt among members.

Special Sessions is the conference mode most international institutions adopt. Scrupulous investigation and hard-hitting report must show the Human Rights Council as preventive in purpose and not just reactive to infringement. Ideally, such a congress will hear evidence, pronounce judgements in resolutions and see to the framing of action plans. Useful deliberations no doubt but it has seemed to strike some participants, again in relation to terrorist outrage, that political issues in violent protest are best dealt with case by case and not by generalised discussion.

Universal Periodic Review, an imaginative innovation, is, as the names implies, an accounting of states' success in the guaranteeing of essential rights. How far has Country X fulfilled its obligations? Will not the use of recognised assessment criteria clearly reveal progress or the lack of it in establishing the priority of human rights? A UN Member State must stand ready for inspection. Out of 192 states a number will be chosen each year to be reviewed. Those failing satisfactory assessment will be condemned in Special Sessions and meet with the continuing concern of the Special Procedures inspectors. Keen attention is to be paid, again in the instance of combating terrorism, to the goings on in Iran, Pakistan and Afghanistan, where terrorist suspects have been granted some asylum. Signs of moving forward are encouraging yet some road blocks will be difficult to remove. There is still the old conundrum whereby 'fighters for freedom', for minority independence, are labelled 'terrorists' by intolerant administrations quick to deny that dissidents have any rights at all. Turkey, an original member of the Commission, blasts away at Kurdish villages. Israel regards breakaway Palestinian activists as intolerable, terrorist neighbours.

Why was it that Israel and the United States felt unable to join a scheme for restructuring the UN's human rights body and breathing life into it? There has been worldwide interest and support. Tel Aviv's reluctance is usually couched in question form. Why are we in Israel so often censured while Arab terror is referred to in coded language or downplayed? Is there always to be a misplaced, relentless criticism of Israel at the expense of action against states with poor human rights records? We might even be considered a 'permanent agenda item'. Did not former UN Secretary-General Kofi Annan, in December 2006, term this anti-Israeli focus 'disproportionate' and 'most unhelpful'? As Council members could we really put up with being victimised with inflammatory rhetoric and one-sided politically resolutions?

Washington's perspectives have been wider and cooler. The State Department regrets the extent of apparent concentration on Israel over against less attention to serious cases of human rights abuse in countries such as Iran, Cuba, Zimbabwe, Burma, Sudan, North Korea and Syria. President George W. Bush, with his War on Terror very much in mind, has declared that the United States will work more effectively outside the Council for the time being until its procedural imbalance and weakness are remedied. Then, the United States would consider Council membership. Meanwhile, the Council will receive generous dollar support.

Not only in Washington is there a constant watch to see how far Geneva can maintain credibility through all-round, urgent reform. Partisan bloc voting must go. States must demonstrate absolute observance of basic human rights and freedoms. Measures of supervision implicit in Special Procedures and the Universal Periodic Review will benefit greatly from having a definite input from international experts.

The International Court of Justice

At the inception of the International Court of Justice (ICJ) in 1945, the UN determined to set up a court which would function as a judicial tribunal to decide disputes between states and give advisory opinion according to international law. At the outset, in the mid-1940s, a world community, reeling from global war, was looking for a reconstituted, ordered framework for handling international relations. Increasingly, as old political associations (many imperial) fractured and new nations emerged often 'fighting for freedom' the Court became more concerned with conflict and arbitration and with the consequences of some regimes denying their people justice. The imposition of sanctions would be the most punitive of enforcing mechanism. At present the ICJ President is the eminent British international lawyer, Dame Rosalyn Higgins.

Towards the end of 2008 there were 12 cases awaiting ICJ judgements. Many cases so far have had to do with contention between states over territorial, environmental and human rights issues. Apropos terrorism there have been two interesting cases, generally referred to as the Nicaragua versus United States and the Lockerbie cases. In 1986, over Nicaragua, the Court found the United States to have violated international law by supporting 'Contra' guerrillas who had spread terror and mined harbours. The United States replied to this by arguing that the ICJ lacked jurisdiction. They would walk away from the Court. Finally, the ICJ ruled in favour of Nicaragua and against the United States who were now to pay reparations. In 1991 Libya's Government was called upon to extradite two Libyans accused by Britain of the terrorist bombing of Pan Am Flight 103 which crashed at Lockerbie in Scotland. Libya refused. Ten years of court work and diplomatic activity ensued prior to judgement in 2001, after hearings of the case in Scotland and the Netherlands. One suspect was freed, the other given life imprisonment. An appeal by the remaining suspect was disallowed.

Ever since its birth the Court has been at pains to stress the linkage of freedoms with responsibilities. In the case of a state, rights, duties and obligations are meshed in an intricate web, the prelude to interdependent not independent action. Nowhere is this more true than in the express injunction over the last 30 years which binds states to refrain from encouraging or tolerating acts of terrorism either elsewhere or, even, within their own borders. There is to be no partiality towards insurgents in other lands. This would be considered 'subversive intervention', a fine sentiment in theory. But as everyone knows the sentiment holds no credibility in conflict-racked Middle East and Asia.

A final point about the UN's monitoring of rights compliance is to recognise the ongoing reverberations of unofficial and unrecorded discussion as delegates meet with their newspapers and conference briefings. The Security Council and General Assembly bring together people with both ingrained preference for fair autonomy and a readiness to listen to others, opportunity and time permitting. They may have just flown in from a terrorist bombing or assassination. The need now to harness efforts to contain terrorism is bringing delegates into the assemblies of the UN much more ready to sink differences and scout for solution. The principles, the ideals, are acting as a leaven.

Conventions, courts and consensus

Something of the search for agreement and legitimacy with Convention to hand, so clear at the UN, is gripping officials' minds in Europe, the Americas, Africa and Asia. Europe has led the running: in early days a European Court of Human Rights was founded in Strasbourg. The work done in 60 years by this Court has expanded enormously as more nations join the European institutions and come into contact with Europe's litigation. The Strasbourg Court has the dual role of carrying a load of cases for judgement and arbitration as well as responsibility for providing legal advice when requested. These responsibilities are crucial since existing human rights provisions are often couched in rather general terms: more precisely states' obligations are made known through the Court's interpretations and setting of precedents. These will then influence the way in which the obligations become understood around the world. They earn the Court's rulings credibility and acceptance.

Case work currently being undertaken ranges over such human rights matters as detention of terrorist suspects, interrogation techniques, imprisonment, expatriation and rendition. Much effort will go into persuading governments to consider 'proportionality'. This requires that there be no interference with fundamental rights unless that is absolutely vital in order to achieve a specific purpose set out in the Convention. At the present time of actual and hypothetical terrorist threat the way in which so many governments chip away at fundamental rights is highly controversial. Impartial lawyers' advice does help but it may not divert politicians' urge to apply tough controls.

The European Union

As for Europe's Convention and Court it is important to note that the Council of Europe, which established them both, should not be confused with the Council of the European Union. The European Union (EU) is not a party to the Convention and has no role in the administration of the European Court of Human Rights. The EU, successor to the European Economic Community (EEC), is a large, growing union of 27 European countries with headquarters in Brussels.

The EU as a political and economic entity is directly concerned with terrorism, more so every year. In 2006 alone there were almost 500 terrorist acts across its extent. To address such problems meetings are frequent. There is an elaborate, detailed set of counter-terrorism strategies which will be looked at in some detail in Chapter 3. The EU has taken to heart fundamental human rights principles above all in the design and promulgation of the Charter of Fundamental Rights of the European Union made final in December 2007. Three constituent bodies in the EU had decided, seven years earlier, in fact, such a charter, 'a solemn proclamation', would be an appropriate declaratory format for aims and principles. The text was to be in harmony with the UN's Declaration of Human Rights and with the European Convention on Human Rights. It so happened that during the working phase of charter preparation there were the traumatic events of 9/11, the Madrid bombings of March 2004 and those of London in July 2005. An outline of rights principles could be useful to keep in mind when the tactical planners got down to business.

Although the EU's new Charter is not legally binding it may be taken into account by individual national courts of law. Predictably, some countries, for instance the United Kingdom, feared that if the Charter were to become legally binding then it would create new legal obligations undermining national sovereignty. In fact, this would be an unlikely development but it does illustrate the suspicious and hesitant way in which some nations regard the proclamation of human rights. Looked at more positively, the EU Charter is the latest element in a whole raft of European treaties, declaration, charters, conventions and court rulings concerned explicitly with fundamental freedoms. The European Court of Human Rights is anyway a protective device in many respects and is mindful of human rights abuse and of clashes between principle and practice.

The United States

Americans have put into being a similar assemblage of Commission, Convention and Court to those designed by the UN and in Europe. After the shock of 9/11 there was on every hand among the 35 members of the OAS a compunction to keep close together with counter-terrorism policies, their aims, programmes and legal procedures. An Inter-American Court of Human Rights has been exceedingly busy, continent wide, with rulings to offset terrorists. The Court has not avoided a great deal of criticism for what has been alleged to be over-hasty and over-prescriptive dealings apropos suspects, their detention, charging and incarceration. Were fundamental freedoms not suffering in a search for a watertight means of defending a threatened homeland?

Africa and Asia

Monitoring agencies were introduced here rather later than in Europe and the Americas. As was remarked earlier in this chapter here were masses of people striding out into new fields of independence and experiment, shaking off foreign tutelage and determined to stand tall by any delineation of their rights. These people, unfortunately, in many countries, have had to suffer authoritarian regimes and the confusions that accompany transition from under-development to managed social and economic redevelopment. Humans and their rights have frequently gone to the wall. Sometimes they have been rescued in a fashion by militant groups whose principles and conduct have earned for them the label 'terrorist'. Human rights courts in Africa and Asia have had a lesser role than in the more developed countries, working as they have had to do amid conflict and dispossession where, as Nelson Mandela once put it, principles have been exercised at the end of a barrel of a gun. There is little doubt that the newer nations are intent on arousing and harnessing wide support for rights whose eventual securing cannot be guaranteed. Inching forward pragmatically, national leaders and their advisors turned to the UN, the EU and inter-American thinking and instructed their lawyers to fashion an African court of Human and People's Rights in January 2005. Comprehensiveness in scope and name marked their concern; it all seems most appropriate to Africans looking over their shoulders at what has been and could be and must now be.

Principles, principles, principles

A discussion of the shaping and promulgation of human rights principles might usefully conclude with some thoughts from Mary Robinson. A doughty campaigner for rights and freedoms and a lawyer, she was President of Ireland from 1990 to 1997 and more recently the UN's High Commissioner for Human Rights from 1997 to 2002. Quite often Mary Robinson has met from others the charge that there is little point in too much reflection on principles of human rights if these are so often transgressed. The principles should help the sorting out of aims and objectives but strategies and programmes are to be organised with more workaday priorities in mind. This is not the view of Mary Robinson. When she relinquished her High Commissioner post she was quoted in *The Boston Globe* of 19 September 2002 thus:

Human rights are now firmly on the agenda of the international community. If one thinks back twenty years to arguments about whether human rights were universal, whether they could be made operational, whether they have a serious place in the conduce of international relations, one would have to conclude that human rights have come a long way . . . There is now much greater recognition of the centrality of human rights and of the immense benefits a rights-based approach brings.

Why, then, she asked, on another occasion, are certain governments 'using the language of combating terrorism to clamp down on legitimate dissent, to be much tougher on human rights defenders . . . ? She emphasises that it is possible to fight terrorism 'while fully upholding human rights. There is a provision, for example, for seeking derogation from certain obligations in times of national emergency. Great Britain has done it . . .'

Principles in the view of the ex-High Commissioner are there to govern our actions but they may be modifiable . . . 'Both contemporary human rights and humanitarian law allow states a reasonably wide margin of flexibility to combat terrorism without contravening human rights and humanitarian legal obligations.' This is where international collaboration and sensitive, realistic programming can operate positively and judiciously. Otherwise, as a former UN Secretary-General, Kofi Annan pointed out, 'we deliver victory to terrorists no act of theirs could achieve'.

3

The state of play; observance or no?

T his chapter is still concerned with the principles of fundamental human rights but more particularly with the practice of observing them. An alternative title for this chapter might be 'With the best intentions'. This has to do with notes of assurance from those in government offices, sitting there with worried brows and unsteady consciences. Of course, they declare, we will act with the best of intentions. They will most certainly hold to the array of fundamental human rights principles that the UN persuaded so many governments to ratify and go on to honour. This is not at all easy; in the face of a challenge to a government on the ground, action demands prompt decision and ordering of priorities. If the challenge is that of general or episodic violence directed against a community then the government has a pre-eminent responsibility to protect and defend their people. More generally, out in the world, there are two universals to reckon with, the validity of human rights consensually agreed and the menace of unrelenting, terrorist violence. Governments must look both ways. As players they determine the state of play, the resultant of their far-from-easy decision.

Standing up to the threat

Definition of the threat must surely come first. What do most people understand by terrorism? A well-worn definition (though there are many) originates with the UN:

Terrorism is the premeditated and illegitimate threat or use of violence by subnational groups or clandestine individuals intended to intimidate or coerce governments, to promote political, religious or ideological outcomes, and to inculcate fear among the public at large.

> Almost every word there throws up a question. 'Premeditated' – can the threat be predictable? What about spontaneous impulses? 'Illegitimate' – in whose eyes, and what are the consequences? As for intimidation and coercion – again how do they happen and what are the results? Considering this definition, and numerous others, it seems vital to think about the springs of motivation like poverty, frustration and the ill-treatment of a minority. And to think also of the sacrificial element that persuades the suicide bomber.

> Some definitions do not always help us with meaning and the appropriate response. As I have written in the companion volume to this book, *Terrorism: Understanding the Global Threat.* Pearson 2007, pp. 12–13.

For the terrorist, the word 'terrorism' may be a misnomer. The actions of those dedicated to a cause may be seen by others as destructive and perverse but for those who believe in what they are trying to achieve the end justifies the means. Here, once more, we meet with a generalisation that fogs a clear meaning. The sheer variety of terrorist campaigning down the centuries throws light sometimes on idealists desperate to overthrow a tyrant or struggling to bring about at least some degree of respect and tolerance, a better deal, for the dispossessed and disenfranchised. Exasperation leads to turbulence and violence. Elsewhere, the idealist is balked at every turn and resorts eventually to destructive and inhumane action. Most terrorists claim to be delivering a political message. All too often their methods go further than the question and answer of political dialogue and they come to depend, however reluctantly, upon thrusting only an answer at opponents. For most political activists, among Palestinians, in Latin America and (formerly) in apartheid South Africa, there has always been the vision of a more secure and beneficial future. Such is the consuming faith of liberators who are fighting for freedom from dictators or imperial rule. In other cases, it is the past which transmits a myth, of invincibility, or of their right to live as they prefer. Terrorism is not a term that terrorists own to: for the main part their intentions and actions define a duty they feel they must discharge. Generally, they are anxious to claim responsibility for what they do.

As for the standardising of any particular definition, the term 'terrorism' undoubtedly has different associations for those responsible for public order, peace and security, for onlookers watching television or reading newspapers and for victims and their relatives. Accordingly, contrasts in perception will have some influence on remedial action. Certainly, there are political and legal differences in perception. David Meltzer (2002) believes that firm definition is virtually unobtainable, 'Terrorism is nowhere fully defined as a legal term . . . The legal vagueness of the word "terrorist" means that traditional means of determining guilt in guilty acts and thoughts are useless because the guilty act is so-ill defined'. Keith Hayward and Wayne Morrison (2002) see definition (and definers) 'caught between the narratives of crime and war'.

In discussion numerous Third World states insist that national liberation struggles do not constitute terrorism. Force is often understood today to be a legitimate means of bringing about regime change or independence in Algeria, Angola, Equatorial Guinea, Namibia, Niger, Somalia, Sudan and Western Sahara, as it also was in Northern Ireland and apartheid South Africa. Death and destruction are the sorry consequence of a righteous initiative being pushed too far or being met by uncomprehending resistance.

How far do we go?

In view of the principles of freedom of thought, opinion, association and political and religious adherence it will never be easy for a concerned and uncertain government to judge just how far to go in matters of 'proportionate control', where, again, if steps are too lax or too strict, order, peace and security may be compromised, if not endangered. Estimating how far to stretch action will require, at crisis times, an administrator capable of judging the extent to which individual rights should yield to safeguard the health and safety of persons in the community. Importantly, he must convince others that his lines of action are ethically sound and practicable. These are significant issues in the light of terrorist incidents like 9/11 in New York in 2001, 7/7 in London in 2005 and the recent supposed aircraft bombing in Britain 1 August 2006 when authority response was widely considered to show elements which are sweepingly coercive and indiscriminate.

In advance of the threat of terrorist malevolence, a counter-terrorism scheme must have a threshold that is clear and candid and has an understandable evaluation of objectives, problems, options and risks. What are the underlying values at stake? That way, a strategy can take shape. That way is the movement now visible in London, Washington, Paris, Berlin, Madrid, Singapore and Canberra.

Government response in most of these places seems to prefer two different lines of counter-terrorist action, a distinction not always talked about in public by the strategists, namely, 'anti-terrorism' and 'counter-terrorism'. Anti-terrorism relies greatly on judicial measures, the force of law. There is an inbuilt danger that such force, if heavily applied, may seriously violate the legal and human rights of suspects and their dependents. (In the matter of so-termed suspects there is considerable anxiety in liberal quarters over a pre-emptive legal approach in many lands.) Counter-terrorism moves directly into physical prevention and restraint and naturally threatens the rights of privacy, movement and association. Of course, both of these lines may be followed in the wake, quite literally, of a foot in the door. In any case, these lines of action are tactical ploys subservient to some overall strategic plan.

Designing a strategy

Most governments are rather coy in revealing the design stages of their counter-terrorist strategies. However, it is possible to get a fair idea of the counter-terrorist strategies that many countries employ by scanning UN and government pronouncements, media discussion and a range of reports from various conferences and workshops. There is so much detail in these strategies and the implications are so far-reaching that it is only possible to sketch the main lines of approach in this chapter. (Once more, readers can chase the detail for themselves with Internet assistance. The 'free encyclopedia', Wikipedia, has a most useful and detailed survey of state planned responses to terrorism under the heading of 'Counter-Terrorism'. Also, the websites of Human Rights Watch and of Liberty are comprehensive and helpful.)

The UN strategy

Twelve months after 9/11 the then Secretary-General, Kofi Annan, unwrapped the UN's intensive design work on an overall counter-terrorism scheme. Fundamentals were clear in that 'the design and enforcement of means to fight terrorism should be carried out in strict adherence with international human rights obligations'. Three main principles were in the forefront of planning. Preventive measures on a cooperative basis were to be in accordance with the UN Charter. A search for legal precision must hold whenever possible to moral norms and values. Protection of vulnerable civilians must be a cardinal concern since most terrorism was indiscriminate.

The Security Council put flesh on objectives with Resolution 1373 passed two days after 9/11, which put in being a Counter-Terrorism Committee (CTC). Their agenda was to be an ambitious one: terrorist funding, post-incident relief schemes, coordinated tracking of specific terrorist groups, investigation of terrorist Internet propaganda and civilian protection in liaison with states' defence departments. Five 'Ds' would be elements in a 'principled, comprehensive strategy' to fight terrorism: *dissuading* disaffected groups from terrorism; *denying* terrorists the means to carry out attacks; *deterring* states from supporting terrorists; *developing* states' capacity to prevent terrorism; *defending* human rights.

The Security Council remit and scheme have not, however, escaped quite sharp criticism from Human Rights Watch. In August 2004 their briefing paper 'Hear No Evil See No Evil' laid fingers on what were regarded as serious deficiencies in the UN approach. True global leadership would require the Security Council to press governments to take much more decisive, concerted action, especially over the financing of terror and the sharing of cross-border information. It took almost three years for the CTC to be strengthened as an Executive Directorate with much enhanced capabilities.

For the Security Council to spend much of its time as a forum where self-serving governments meet is seen by Human Rights Watch as inadequate. Should the United States get away with procrastination and lame rejoinders as to the priority of home-land security over rights adherence? Would it help if the CTC, for example, paid more attention to what states advanced as their prospective programmes for counter-terrorism, rather than checking their actual achievements? The suggestion is that UN coordinators appointed by the Security Council should expect of UN Members regular, factual accounts of what place they gave human rights in their countering programmes. They would also have to explain any neglect of those rights. If this were so, the United States would have to answer for its unilateral, deliberate disregard of elemental rights.

Several other examples of rights of violation, in the view of Human Rights Watch, could have been handled much more smoothly and incisively by an alert Security watchdog. Egypt's long history of using anti-terrorist decrees to put down even peaceful protest has worsened since 9/11. Military tribunals and emergency edicts deal with anyone bold enough to engage in strikes, demonstrations and public meetings. Morocco's surveillance and hunting of Islamic groups thought to be linked to al-Qaida has increased dramatically since 12 suicide attacks back in May 2003. An estimated five thousand people were rounded up to be detained without trial and very likely tortured. Malaysia's national security arrangements are related to a draconian law, passed in 1960, in response to Communist insurgency. Today, it is used as a blanket suppressive of many basic human rights. To evident CTC surprise in June 2002 Sweden, that liberal bastion, was found guilty of violations. Several terrorist suspects were forcibly returned to Egypt. According to reliable press reports the suspects were roughly handled at the airport in Stockholm and there were US security personnel looking on. This was 'rendition' (see Chapter 8). There was a well-founded fear that the evicted would be ill-treated in their home country, for Egypt had long used forms of torture in police routine investigative work. To the discredit of the CTC the Swedish reports on these cases, sounding a note of transparent justification, were not taken up with much vigour. And it was not until May 2005 that the UN Committee against Torture noted that Sweden had violated the absolute prohibition on torture by forcing the Egyptian nationals to go home.

At this point one enters the lively controversy over whether states may be culpable for terrorism. Should not states using harsh counter-terrorism methods be judged against international moral and socio-political conventions? There are many instances of state counter-terrorism going over the humanitarian edge. In December 2006 the Israeli Supreme Court ruled that targeted (specifically named) killing is a lawful form of self-defence against terrorists. It is thought that the United States' CIA had Cuba's Fidel Castro very literally in an assassin's sights. The United Kingdom, dealing with Northern Ireland's 'Troubles', had only very slight reservations in its heavy-handed all-things-go response to the Irish Republican Army (IRA). Syria, Colombia, Spain, Malaysia, Pakistan and the United States, on occasion, have all used tactics to do with surveillance, arrest, detention, forced confession and imprisonment that absolutely have violated the human rights agenda. Many of these practices attend still today. Certainly, most liberal criticism centres on those state practices aiming at general 'squashing' of terrorists rather than at all costs some selective, analytical approach to terrorist motivation and the circumstances surrounding their use of violence.

The UN counter-terrorism strategy continues to acquire more momentum. Over the last decade UN spokesperson have frequently deplored the circumvention of the law's due process and the secrecy that accompanies restrictive controls. They find abhorrent the widespread profiling of Muslims on racial and religious grounds. Tough repression in so many countries has been curtailing almost all human rights – civil, political, economic, social and cultural. Certain rights, it is stressed, must not be subject to 'derogation'. That is, there can be no let out for their not being kept in place. Louder calls are constantly voiced for systematic, expert examination of the root causes of terrorism, causes that have to do with socio-economic problems and ethnic alienation. Again, in more sombre fashion, the UN has commissioned advisory groups to look into what perhaps lies around the corner, namely, the catastrophic onset of nuclear and biological terrorism. Yet, something more was seen as urgently needed, something in the shape of a consensual strategy in which all the 192 UN Member States could participate. At last, in September 2006 the General Assembly adopted a Global Counter-terrorism Strategy.

The Strategy took the form of a Resolution (rather a wordy, general-in-tone one, perhaps inevitably) together with a detailed Plan of Action (very much in businesslike terms). Here was a mega-scheme writ large for immediate, extensive action to bring on board all 192 UN Members to deal with a world problem, that of terrorism. Four pillars of action were to be crucial lines to success:

■ Measures to address factors conducive to the spread of terrorism;

- Measures to prevent and combat terrorism;
- Measures to build states' capacity to prevent and combat terrorism;
- Measures to ensure respect for human rights and the rule of law as fundamental in the fight against terrorism.

Here was an ambitious agenda with more than 50 practical recommendations and provisions for action over the next decade.

Responsibility for implementing the scheme is that of UN Member States. In addition, a seminal role is played by the UN system itself. The Counter-terrorism Committee of the UN, as we have mentioned, foresaw coordination of action as imperative and was instrumental in setting up in July 2005 a Counter-terrorism Implementation Task Force. A very comprehensive Task Force database would compile information about counter-terrorism activities undertaken or planned by 24 UN departments, specialised agencies and programmes. UN searching of this material would give some idea of achievements and of areas to be given prime attention.

Conditions conducive to the spread of terrorism are to be addressed through strengthening existing programmes on conflict prevention, negotiation, mediation, conciliation, peacekeeping and peacebuilding. The link between the traditional development agenda essentials of poverty reduction and socio-economic development and the fight against terrorism will be highlighted. Perhaps an innovation here was to accentuate another area of concern, namely, the needs of victims and the vulnerable in places dubbed 'fragile' and with 'terrorism potential'. Fieldwork and funding is already obvious in some 90 countries.

The US strategy

One of the most interesting accounts of counter-terrorism strategies is that of Shirley Lum Kennedy, *The Effectiveness of Counter-*

terrorism (2002) published by the US Department of State (cf. their website). Fairly clearly the basis for Washington's operation planning takes account of the conventional, three-element definition of terrorism, that is, motivation-opportunity-capability. Terrorist networks such as al-Qaida and their confederated associates as well as lone individuals and small groups generally attempt to 'aggregate' local grievances into ideological concerns. Widening a grievance and heightening it will motivate others to join in proposed action. This thinking reads a trifle simplistically, perhaps, given the variability and unpredictability of so much terrorism. Nevertheless, this line of consideration leads on to a proposed US response to a threefold threat complex. There will be leaders who inspire, guide and direct. There will be safe havens providing physical space and ideological space to facilitate freedom of action and, nowadays, cyberspace channelling information and intelligence collection. There will be the underlying conditions where grievance and conflict provide fertile soil and 'fuel' for extremists.

It is not spelled out in this strategy but it must have been in the mind of the State Department that multiple attacks on the threefold threat complex risk basic human rights if targeted people are seen as 'terrorists' and so, in military terms, are 'expendable'. A successful and ethically sound strategy will keep human rights and needs to the forefront when it undertakes work designed to improve those 'underlying conditions' that motivate hyperviolent protest. In any case, Washington acknowledges that strategic initiatives are most effectively translated into action through regional schemes.

What's happening out there?

American counter-terrorism strategists need to keep a 24-hour watch across the Atlantic. Several countries are reputed to sponsor terrorism among their neighbours, Iran and Syria notably. There is no doubt, as Washington admits, that international intervention in Iraq, spearheaded by the United States, is used by terrorists for radicalisation all over the Middle East. In Afghanistan, the insurgent hold of Taliban is being eased but for any counter-initiative to make permanent sense there has to be visible dealing with legitimate grievances, democratic administration housed in provincial centres and an alternative to narcotics cultivation. Elsewhere, the Israeli–Palestinian conflict, the Israeli building of a wall between Israelis and Arabs and the contest between Hamas and Hizbullah, the tensions in Gaza and Lebanon, all call for restoration of fundamental rights – the sort of diplomatic minefield that requires great awareness and sensitivity in countering recourse to violence. Somehow, a workable strategy has to be designed against the pull of half a hundred imponderables.

What is also happening out there is change in structure and in logistics, so it is thought in the State Department. A trend is discernible towards 'guerilla terrorism' where al-Qaida, for instance, targets and trains dissident nationals in various countries. This increasingly reshapes terrorism and sharpens the focus on locating sponsors-at-a-distance. A list is kept of 'foreign terrorist organisations' (FTOs), currently numbering 34, and of their reputed sponsors. There now seems to be a greater reliance by activists on disseminating misinformation and anti-Western propaganda via broadcasting and the Internet. Both of the changes need to be addressed through a 'hearts and minds' approach in Europe, the Middle East, Africa and Asia. The United States with so many of its expeditionary forces in these places is rather slowly beginning to realise this. No military component will do that job: countering terrorists is to be done in peaceful mode through thought, work and deed. In slightly technical terms the US State Department will give the task forces the aim of 'disaggregating a threat'. This appears to refer to countering work – against propaganda, subversion and breaking the link in the protest chain that exploits ordinary people's discontent and manipulates them towards violence. This is large language, difficult and time-consuming to realise.

Essentially, task forces will be in the field regionally. Theirs will be the job of creating 'trusted networks' of supportive governments, private citizens, NGOs, and multilateral institutions to help, over time, to wean at-risk populations away from seductive appeals. Needs, rights and opportunities are to be prominent in common discussion and insurgency will eventually wither.

Worth looking at in some detail on account of premise and promise, the US State Department strategy is pitched at a demanding level. Representing a peaceful, democratic set of initiatives it stands, one might think, rather forlornly, beside the loud, stern, weapons-ready counter measures the United States has traditionally employed. There are signs of beginning interest in the human width and depth of the US strategy in South-east Asia, Europe and Latin America.

What's happening at home?

Designing an appropriate counter-terrorism strategy called for system changes not only abroad but at home. Abroad, and, over the last 10 years, prominent in the American press are the assurances of Messrs Bush and Rice, particularly, that the United States will never lower vigilance to see human rights sustained. One reads of US overseas development programmes where human rights protection is a vital component.

Reality makes for anxiety and controversy. What of the close relationship to many countries with poor human rights in Asia and around the Mediterranean? In the struggle to cope with terrorist activity how 'clean' are the rights records of US associates in Pakistan, Malaysia, Philippines, China, Kyrgyzstan and Uzbekistan? Spokesmen for the US Administration now and then try to justify these alignments, distasteful to many, since a 'weak' state might provide a base from which a terrorist cell could operate. States judged able to balance politico-military 'realities' with a degree of idealism and ethics are robust allies in meeting terrorism, actual or possible.

As for 'homeland security' and away from the fine, humane phrasing in the strategy why does security depend upon rounding up thousands of 'suspect citizens'? Why the gross interference with privacy and liberty? Do Americans really deserve those cameras everywhere, the baggage checks, the everyday stop-on-demand? Granted that the horror of 11 September 2001 was so traumatic, it appears to have tipped the balance disproportionately towards security at all costs with human rights observance trailing in the rear.

Alongside the wordy rationale of the strategy there was to be swift hoisting into place of appropriate tactics. Federal legislation would have a prime supportive place. Seven days after the September outrage the Unites States Patriot Act was placed before Congress. It was cleverly framed as an Act for 'Uniting and Strengthening America by Providing Appropriate Tools Required to Intercept and Obstruct Terrorism'.

The Act allowed the FBI to put wiretaps on suspects and to permit unspecified interception of Internet browsing and emailing. Search warrants could be levied without warning. Any group 'seeking to influence the policy of government by 'intimidation or coercion' would be proscribed. Attempts to fund anything conceived of as terrorist in intent would be clamped down.

Civil rights groups, aghast at the closing down of an open society, raised impassioned protest at the compromising of a wide range of public and private liberties. There seemed to be an element of demonology in the President's remark in 2003 that it was simply 'not practicable' to try terrorist suspects under constitutional rules and legal principles. After all, as Bush saw it, his country was 'at war with terrorism', and even a suspect would be termed an 'enemy combatant'. This new category remains unrecognised in international law. Individuals detained with such a label round their necks do not have the protection of US domestic law nor access to legal representation. They are likely to be extracted from the criminal justice system and to be transferred to a military base.

Since 2005 draft legislation 'to enhance domestic security' has authorised, among other things, arbitrary and secret arrests and deportation hearings for suspects held by the military. Particularly worrying to liberal lawyers is another category, that of 'non-citizens'. Many of the people so named are from the Middle East and South Asia, recent immigrants whose earlier associations or behaviour are of 'special interest' to the US Department of Justice. Their complicity in 'terrorist intent' was not easily proved and many of them were then held under immigration laws, which, in a number of respects, stand aside from conventional court process routines. Even more irregular was the uncaring way in which several thousand of these unfortunates were interrogated without any access to counsel. Subsequently many of them have been incarcerated for long periods without charge.

It is the plight of the hundreds confined at Guantanamo Bay, Cuba that has aroused the strongest disapproval around the world. Many of the detainees are not US citizens and they have been taken in Afghanistan or arrested on suspicion of being al-Qaida members. Shamefully, these prisoners are denied the external protection of international law and UN conventions. They are held incommunicado and no tribunal has been permitted access to men who in other circumstances might have been categorised as prisoners of war and so subject to the support of the Geneva Convention. Even the Inter-American Commission on Human Rights was prepared to get clarification of the men's status. Cuba, of course, is outside US sovereign territory but it seems as though the United States cannot always honour so many of the fundamental rights that brought renown to the Founding Fathers of the American Constitution.

The UK strategy

The United Kingdom's scheme for counter-terrorism all the time raises a multiplicity of issues. It is only possible here to touch on a selection of the problems that provoke most controversy. In March 2003 Human Rights Watch had this to say about the United Kingdom's aims and methods:

In the United Kingdom the government's response to the events of September 11 resulted in laws, policies and practices that undermine fundamental human rights protections, including the right to seek asylum and prohibitions against arbitrary detention and mistreatment. The UK derogated from the European Convention on Human Rights (ECHR), the sole Council of Europe member to do so on counter-terrorist grounds. Subsequent government action and rhetoric signaled a further tendency to opt out of human rights obligations, with little effort to find accommodation between national security interests and the protection of human rights . . .

A rather damning conclusion this and there is scant sign that the position has improved. Naturally during the last few years the country has been shaken that terrorists have so ruthlessly blasted their way into the perceptions of government and its constituents. Londoners cannot forget July 2005 when a terrorist cell, very likely linked to al-Qaida, carried out a series of suicide bombings on the Underground killing 52 and injuring hundreds more. The incident had some similarity to what took place in Madrid in March 2004 when commuter trains were bombed. Then, 181 died and 2,050 were injured.

Public trauma is understandable but surely it does not excuse the cutting of corners by an over-reactive administration. Another Human Rights Watch note is unsettling:

The United Nations Committee alert in December 2001 to the after effects of 9/11 was concerned about British legislative measures in the pipeline which could have far-reaching, negative effects. Committee members registered their anxiety that the United Kingdom might lay aside some of its obligations towards the maintenance of human rights – the procedure known as 'derogation'. Even when the Committee met representatives from Britain the latter had forcefully made the point that their obligations to the United Nations Counter-terrorism Committee under Resolution 1373 took precedence over their obligations towards the Human Rights Committee.

This double dealing must have made a bad impression as to London's straightforwardness and honesty.

The United Kingdom's position over the detention of terrorist suspects has aroused a good deal of controversy both at home and overseas. Legislation was rushed through Parliament in the United Kingdom so that in December 2001 the Anti-Terrorism, Crime and Security Act (ATCSA) became law. This, in the main, provides for indefinite detention without charge or trial of non-UK nationals suspected of terrorism-related activities. Britain's Home Secretary is to certify a person under scrutiny either as a suspected terrorist or as a national security risk. Evidence as to complicity will be kept secret with no access to it nor may any legal advocate discuss it. How, one wonders, can an adequate defence ever be assembled? Detention certification rests vaguely 'on national security grounds', where threats are hypothetical rather than actual. Only on a point of law may an appeal be lodged. It certainly has not advanced objectivity that London found it necessary to 'derogate' from Article 5 of the European Convention on Human Rights which specifically rules for fair trials. Critics in human rights lobbies have regarded the United Kingdom's position as very different from that under certain authoritarian governments. Even so, they have to admit that media reports in 2001 gave plenty of coverage to a popular mood where derogation would be the least of sins.

Detention legislation has sometimes almost 'hit the buffers'. In December 2004, for instance, the House of Lords Judicial Committee ruled that indefinite detention was incompatible with the United Kingdom's own Human Rights Act 1998. There are 16 basic rights in the Act all taken from the European Convention of Human Rights. Whitehall had to think and act quickly. Two alternatives to indefinite detention were brought in. First, so-called Control Orders would regulate and restrict movement. (More will be said about these later.) Second, 'diplomatic assurances' would cover deported nationals who might be at risk of harm on their return. The alternative was stressed by the Government pointing out that UN Members had underwritten an express prohibition of 'refoulement' where persons might be returned to countries noted for their harsh treatments. Had London overlooked the fact that way back in October 1996 four EU states, Italy, Poland, Slovakia and Lithuania, were stoutly standing by their position that a human right, not to be tortured, for example, needed to be balanced against the national security interests of the state. Very possibly because the UK Government could sense that procedural safeguards would prove inadequate, negotiations were struck up with a number of states with poor human rights records, Algeria, Tunisia, Lebanon and Egypt, in the hope that they would see to the well-being of any deportees sent there. Questions remained. Would blanket diplomatic assurances suffice? Would courts in the United Kingdom back the assurances when a suspect appealed against a detention order?

There has been some sort of sideways movement on these problems recently; in late 2005 when the European Parliament in Brussels argued that in the case of an asylum seeker the applicant should have right of appeal against a state's refusal to admit them. In this way there would be a right to rebut presumptions of safety if one were transferred abroad. Could not those deported nationals expect a similar benefit? It has to be said, though, that asylum seekers cannot expect much in the way of welcome from Britain. Legislation is discriminating with clauses in the ATCSA (2001) and the far from warm-hearted Immigration, Nationality and Asylum Act 2002 that undermine markedly the right to seek asylum ostensibly in the interests of national security. There seems to be a climate of suspicion about nefarious intent. Frequent articles about this in the press and fairly consistent attitudes on the Opposition benches in the House of Commons attest to the backing of a 'No, not here' demand.

Two government provisions in counter-terrorism in the United Kingdom at the moment lead to great heat in debate. Control Orders excite much controversy. The criminalising of the 'glorification' and 'encouragement' of terrorism is the other burning issue.

Control Orders were created as a consequence of the Prevention of Terrorism Act 2005 in response to a House of Lords' ruling against existing detention procedures. Government justifications were prominently reported in the press. An example of this is a letter to *The Guardian* of 24 December 2007 from Tony McNulty MP (Minister of State for Security, Counter-terrorism, Crime and Policing – note the title!) where he writes that Control Orders are used only in a limited number of carefully selected cases, 'tailored' to risks posed by the individual concerned. Strong safeguards protect human rights. Where the controlled person cannot see evidence against them, it is for security reasons and only an appointed legal representative may do any inspection. Each Control Order receives a mandatory review by the High Court. Finally, these orders are a necessary and proportionate response to current threats as McNulty writes:

Not everybody would feel reassured by this view. Once more, the human rights lobbies, sometimes accused of being 'soft on terror', have pointed to what they consider to be failures to support rights fully. Indeed, they go so far as to see the orders undermining a number of very necessary safeguards such as presumption of innocence, the right to a fair trial, the right to have access to evidence. Are these orders not some sort of indefinite measure still in the grip of secrecy? It is virtually a type of house arrest where any controlled person who breaches the surveillance routine by failing to report daily is in danger of arrest on a criminal charge. By far the most penalising feature of these orders is thought to be the fact that the controlled can have no clear idea of precisely what they are supposed to have done or how legal procedures will operate. If the controlled person decides to appeal for withdrawal of the Order or for its modification the Home Secretary will consider it but is only likely to uphold the appeal if it is commonly thought that the evidence is flawed. The chances of that happening are slim.

Interestingly, in the United Kingdom both the High Court and the Court of Appeal are unhappy with the Government's scheme, seeing it as incompatible with human rights law. Any sort of house arrest impinges on man's right to liberty unless there are incontrovertible reasons for judicial restraint. Similar views have come from the European Commissioner on Human Rights. If terrorism is seen as a threat to the rule of law and democratic values, he has asked, why do some states respond with legislation which undermines those values? He must have a good number of governments in mind.

The other government provisions in the United Kingdom making for controversy are to do with a charge of 'incitement'. The bombing of London in July 2005 certainly gave impetus to discourage terrorist recruitment. Two months before, the Council of Europe had approved that states criminalise 'public provocation to commit terrorist offences whether or not such provocation directly advocates terrorism'. Following this, in September 2006, Whitehall set about criminalising also a new offence of 'encouraging, justifying or glorifying, terrorism'. London mosques supposed to be fomenting extreme views were closed and their imams detained. Did this not clearly criminalise free speech, non-violent expression and religious worship, it was asked, even where there was no intention to commit violence? Even more debatably, 'unacceptable behaviour' was added to the list of grounds for deportation or exclusion of foreigners.

Justifying the hardening of counter-terrorism lines ministers fall back on the notion of a state of emergency yet on other occasions they repeatedly stress that threats are neither specific nor immediate. One has to allow for those protectors and defenders of the public to follow the line of 'better safe than sorry' so long as responses are appropriate and consistent. 'Proportionate' seems to be the word, that is, effective, democratic, widely understood and accepted. There is a long way to go.

The European Union

One can get some idea of Europe's state of play in counter-terrorism by inspecting press reports, information from such quarters as Human Rights Watch, Amnesty International and various government official statements. The EU is an association of European states, now 27 of them, working for consensus in matters political, economic, social and cultural. It is well worth while looking at the strategy the EU has designed, which is being translated into action, in most respects, by EU Member States.

A number of action plans have been put together and agreed by the EU. The first saw daylight in September 2001 with the US horror in mind. Then in April 2002 Brussels published a Europe Action Plan in the *Fight against Terrorism; the State of Play*. At this point it was considered urgent to seek for cooperation with external partners such as the United States and Russia. The current strategy, a most ambitious undertaking filling out comprehensively the earlier schemes, was adopted by all EU Members on 25 March 2004 as a Declaration on Combating Terrorism.

Presented to Members in 2004 was a long-term strategy to address all factors contributing to terrorism, the nature of threats and their root causes. Member States were 'to act jointly in a spirit of solidarity'. They were already bound to two agreements: the European Convention on the Suppression of Terrorism 1977 and the Council of Europe's European Convention on Human Rights 1953. They also had very firm obligations to stand by 12 counter-terrorism conventions. Actually, the Suppression Convention contained a loophole which remained open for

20 years. Signatories should treat terrorist offences as common crime generally leading to prosecution and extradition. Liaison with other Members would be of help. Yet, it looked as though there was a possibility in the Convention of Members being able to treat some offences as 'political' and so avoid extradition. States carrying out the EU counter-terrorism strategy would need to decide on 'framework decisions' and put them into effect as soon as practicable. Team work would do this most effectively. Means of dealing with exchange of information, the location and freezing of terrorist assets and funding, the protection of civilian public transport, essential services and production facilities, bio-terrorist possibilities, the hot pursuit across borders of suspects were all to be given top priority. Indeed, there has to be the closest possible collaboration between adjacent states for there are no borders within the EU since the single European Act 1993 and no limits to the right of free movement. On the other hand, the external frontiers of the EU such as the Mediterranean and the Channel coast necessitate effective controls. Much effort goes into bilateral agreements to try to deal fairly with a number of temporary immigrants and asylum seekers whose identities and pacific intention need to be confirmed. Security assurance and judicial cooperation would be effected through liaison between law enforcement agencies to permit common definition of offences, with the aim, also, of standardising procedures and penalties. The granting of special powers should be for a limited period only and their nature and consequences need to be intelligible to neighbouring state authorities. Surveillance, early warning systems and alert and response arrangements would bring in Europol for police and forensic duties. They would set up task forces and working parties to provide situation and trend reports and the analysis of actual and possible incidents. An innovative idea was to target action towards Third World countries, under the EU's external relations umbrella, so that counter-terrorism capacities and commitment to combating terrorism there could be enhanced. This would be achieved through two

media: technical assistance via security personnel and foreign developmental programmes to consolidate social and economic self-sufficiency. All the above is detailed in 15 elaborate sections in the EU strategy.

The EU action plans and strategies make for good reading but the critical questions are to do with the firmness and extent of realisation. With 27 sovereign states nominally bound together there is bound to be a gulf between rhetoric and reality and a sensitivity about the discharging of common responsibilities. The US press has been discussing the extent to which a united driving force in Europe is taking up the determination to act against terrorism following the catastrophic events in New York, Madrid and London. In an editorial in June 2007 *The New York Herald Tribune* thought the gearing up of security proposals rather less than optimal. Similar notions have now and then appeared in *The Boston Globe* and *The New York Times* about the 'divisive dynamics' in other countries that do not have the advantage of the North Atlantic Treaty Organisation's (NATO's) consolidating initiatives. On a more official level in June 2005 the US Administration was firm in its approval of the EU's action plans and the 2004 strategy. They 'maximise Europe's counter-terrorism capabilities', it was said.

Spain and Italy have introduced various stringent controls on freedom of expression which have caused newspaper editors and publishing houses a certain amount of concern about illegitimate 'muzzling'. Courts in both countries have brought in penalties to do with 'incitement' and 'provocation' where the furnishing of proof has not been either systematically or objectively sought. Similarly, critics in France have been wondering about the nature of so-called 'criminal association' either in person or through conference or correspondence where indictment is raised now from misdemeanour to felony. French police are able to detain a suspect on the flimsiest of 'preventive' and 'radicalist' accusations and maximum sentences have been notably lengthened. All these three states have put up barriers to asylum seekers from North Africa leading usually to exclusion.

In the case of Spain, for 40 years the Government has had to cope with the Basque separatist movement, Euskadi ta Askatasuna (ETA), who are armed, and with their non-violent, pro-independent followers. Spain's counter-terrorist movement has now broadened to fight both Basque 'terrorists' and 'terrorists' of any other persuasion. Tighter and tighter controls leading to solitary confinement and secret trials are hard-line challenges to Spaniards' freedom of association and expression.

There is perhaps a similar enlargement of counter-terrorism drive in the case of Russia, which is not an EU Member but a country whose like-mindedness has been looked for by Brussels. The independence group there are the 'rebels' in the Caucasian province of Chechnya. Ever since 1999 Moscow has justified its hunting of these separatists as an imperative to fight off terrorists. As everybody has to do. In the course of savage ground battles, aerial bombing and systematic abuse through 'forced disappearances' and extra-judicial executions, civilian casualties have soared. And observation of human rights by each side has been infinitesimal. World leaders have shown little dismay at Russia's campaigning. In many respects they have concurred with former President Putin's claim that the vicious clearing up of the Chechen problem was part of a justified European operation to rid the continent of violent extremists. Once more we have the observance of fundamental human rights sullied by political considerations.

Asia

As Chapter 2 showed, nations, especially those in South-east Asia, have been growing keener to subscribe to the enumeration and observance of human rights with their own Human Rights Charter and careful monitoring of its provisions. Despite a significant amount of political feuding the trench warfare has not altogether dissipated Asia's ethical values and loyalties. Great importance is attached in many parts of Asia to pragmatic rather than moral association with the United States. Giving impetus to counter-terrorist policies is the argument prominent in Washington, Singapore, Jakarta and Manila that 'weak' or 'rogue' states may form or maintain terrorist links. Strength against this will depend on Asia's togetherness backed and infused with US dollars and weaponry.

In pursuit of the rationale outlined above, and as far as one can make out, Washington regards Pakistan and Uzbekistan as key 'front-liners' in the struggle to get rid of the Taliban, al-Qaida and the like. Significant human rights violations have been noted and largely ignored, taking second place to tactical, logistical priorities, though there is some low-key discourse among the allies about restoring the importance of human rights. Indonesia and Malaysia are considered to be 'second-line states'. Democracy in this area is patchy in extent, and inconsistent where it does take hold. Islam counts a large majority of people in this region as loyal adherents but this does not prevent the intrusion of hyper-radical and destructive secular elements. Indonesia's ability to supply dependable information about dissident movements prior to their exploding into violence is seen by the United States as worth more than what might be a rather shallow maintenance of human rights. Malaysia's capacity for hunting dissident cells has led to its receiving both plaudits and dollars and a long-standing secondment of a US security task force. A 'third front' is that of China. US–Chinese relationships have warmed in recent years when both sides stress participation in counter-terrorism as a dutiful business, with China, rather like Russia and Spain, regarding a struggle against separatists as a component in a legitimate, countering strategy.

These are the political calculations of 'interest' somewhat masking the honesty of intention in the safeguarding of human rights. However, in various parts of Asia the picture is not all dispiriting.

The Association of South-East Asian Nations (ASEAN) has had fruitful discussions with the EU over ways and means of forwarding counter-terrorism and has taken part in exploratory talks with Australia, China, New Zealand and South Korea. Naturally ASEAN's diverse membership with fledgling democracies, communist countries and military dictatorships has made decisions on some key issues hard going. Inclusion of Japan and North Korea has made stumbling progress as these highly autonomous states are wary of any external intervention. Dialogue and mediation with other more liberal (and trade-important) states are bringing human rights into sharper focus and a better position. The Asia Human Rights Charter is a step in the proper direction but much more is needed to convince certain states that counter-terrorism depends on the protection and preservation of fundamental liberties. Anything else fuels terrorist endeavour. Combating terrorism requires reaffirming human rights values, not closing them off to one side.

The next chapter will consider what the law and lawmakers can and cannot do to help preserve human rights. Before that it may well be helpful to remember what American statesman Benjamin Franklin said 220 years ago, 'He who would put security before liberty deserves neither . . .'

4

Laws and terrorism: the United Kingdom and the United States

T his is a chapter with a difference. It has been decided to present schematically UK legislation to do with counter-ing terrorism. This is because the interested reader may visit the Home Office website and consult quite easily the mass of material there detailing legislation currently on the statute book, together with a good deal of review. Here we are concerned with the force of law in anti-terrorism. Questions are abundant. How can laws and lawmakers help us in the worldwide battle against terrorists? What sort of laws are most effective? Will the laws that home in on terrorism protect our fundamental rights? First, though, the relevance of international law to UK domestic law will be considered.

International law

Legal authorities, writing about international law, have tradition-ally stressed two basic characteristics. Primarily, international law is an indispensable body of rules, for the most part regulating states' relationships, without which it would be virtually impos-sible to have steady and frequent contact between states. This body of law acknowledges and respects mutual relations and rights. Within this seemingly comfortable framework there are the sovereign states jealously guarding their own autonomies, not too well disposed towards external interference, however well meaning and clearly articulated. In the second place, over the last 100 years nation states have become willing and loyal members of associations such as the League of Nations, the UN and the EU. States have come to recognise the usefulness and discipline of constructing machinery to deal with problems, economic, social and political, all of which have a real salience and urgency. Terrorist activities now stand top of the list of problems. Concerning international attempts to bring about solidarity and legal agreement, many lawyers will point out that state sovereignties represent no more than competencies, however wide, which they enjoy within the limits of international law. That goes a good deal further than 'mutual respect'.

The history of the last decade shows some evidence of heightened concern about extremists and violence and possible responses to them. As long ago as 1934, in connection with the assassination by terrorists of Yugoslavia's King Alexander in Marseilles, Yugoslavia formally accused the Hungarian Government of tacitly conniving in the killing, as it had knowingly allowed major preparations for the deed to be carried out on Hungarian territory. In the course of settling the dispute, the League of Nations affirmed that two duties rested upon every state: neither to encourage nor to tolerate on its territory any terrorist activity with a political purpose. They must do all in their power to prevent terrorism anywhere else and to this end they should lend assistance to any state requesting it. Three years later the League of Nations Council drafted a Convention of the Repression of International Terrorism. This actually never saw light for League Members were unable to define or describe the concept of terrorism. Today, on the other hand, we might not see Alexander's killing as meeting the modern criterion of terrorism. The League's successor, the United Nations, finally succeeded in getting UN Members in the General Assembly (first in 1949 and then in

1971) to support and ratify a Convention to Prevent and Punish Acts of Terrorism.

Modern lawyers make several other points about international law. Reliance on that law focuses on three objectives: (a) to protect the citizens of a state, (b) to forestall, prevent and limit terrorist planning and activities and (c) to give legal authority to counter-terrorist strategies and measures. All of this involves some intervention, where external, authorised action may be carried out within the internal territory of a sovereign state. Not too many years ago this would have been quite impossible. Then, again, there is the conclusion that international law is 'weak law' where its legal machinery is hardly compatible in efficiency with that of most countries generally. An added problem is that difficult-to-reconcile balance between international law and the domestic systems of states. These days, most of these systems in legal parlance are 'dualistic' where the two systems are distinct. New international laws have to be carefully considered to permit ratification commensurate with national law. A few states, Spain, Germany and the Netherlands, for example, have a 'monist' system where the new law can be accepted without too many problems. Canada, Australia and the United States are increasingly inclined to favour monism. International law in a monist system can be directly applied by a national judge and may be invoked by citizens just as if it were national law. In the Netherlands a citizen believing national law violates his human rights may go to a Dutch judge who may then apply, say, the rulings of the International Covenant on Civil and Political Rights even though this lacks compatibility with national law.

The UK approach

Terrorism was a word on many lips in the 1960s and 1970s for in Northern Ireland there was conflict between the IRA and the UK Government. Originating in the 1920s, known as 'The Troubles', this brought gun and bomb to Northern Ireland streets and occasionally to England. London and Belfast saw decision and indecision in Whitehall, when law, to meet unpredictable mayhem, had to move rapidly to prop up a tottering security situation. Government counter-terrorism was widely thought repressive and disproportionate. Those wanted for offences even remotely to do with terrorism could be tried without jury, the law fearing an Irish jury was either partisan or open to persuasion. (Perhaps this contingency arises where accused terrorists are on home ground with sympathisers nearby.)

The spread of terrorist violence into mainland England in those years induced London to furnish security maintenance with a series of preventive parliamentary acts, between 1974 and 1989, on the whole conferring emergency powers upon police when terrorism was suspected. Some consolidation of these acts was brought into being during 1976, 1978 and 1979, following a series of public house bombings, leading to alarm and confusion in English towns. But were we doing the right thing damaging essential 'civil liberty'? Police and soldiers over in Ulster could stop, question, arrest, search and seize. Was this to endanger our freedoms and rights in England? Whether or not questions such as these, frequently noised abroad, were entirely realistic, given the situation's gravity, is arguable. In the end, after 20 years, Parliament at last replaced the acts with a grand definitive measure, the Terrorism Act 2000. The terrorists, so *The Daily Mail* thought in April 2000, were now to be 'nobbled'.

There are now a number of definite and detailed counter-terrorism laws in operation. These are the laws of the years 2000, 2001, 2005 and 2006. To get the whole picture of the legal approach, we need to look very carefully at each of the acts.

Terrorism Act 2000

Not surprisingly, in view of recent history, this Act, in making provisions about terrorism, was to make temporary provision for

Northern Ireland and about 'prosecution and punishment of certain offences, the presence of peace and maintenance of order'. Its applicability has now been extended beyond Ireland. The chief provisions of the Act are as follows:

■ A sound definition of terrorism, making it possible to build a new set of police and investigative powers into terrorist incidents, beyond what was customary for ordinary offences;

■ A list of proscribed international organisations, mostly related to Islamic fundamentalism (an update of this list in 2008 now numbers 34). Group membership or support is sufficient for prosecution;

■ Police given wider stop-and-search powers and authority to arrest and detain suspects without charge for up to 48 hours. This could be extended up to 7 days if further time for investigation were needed;

■ The Home Secretary and police may define any area in the country or any time wherein they can stop and search any vehicle or person and seize articles useful to terrorists;

■ New offences introduced: inciting terrorist acts, seeking or providing training for terrorist purpose at home or abroad, collecting or possessing information of 'a kind likely to be useful to anyone committing or preparing an act of terrorism'.

As expected, there was plenty of public controversy. The definition appeared to list intimidation and public exhortation as indictable. How was terrorist intent to be proved? Stop-and-search power was strongly criticised. Could this be a hangover from Northern Ireland? Now this country had more anti-terrorism legislation on its statute books than almost any other developed democracy. Was the whole of the United Kingdom uniformly threatened by terrorist assault?

A criticism common in 2000 (to be amplified in the case of later legislation) was that certain parts of the Act paved the way for a misguided attack on Islamic extremism. Simplistic portrayal of Islam as 'dangerous' would further alienate and marginalise the very communities in which the Government professed to be fighting radicalism. Would Asians, contrary to the Race Relations Act, be disproportionately stopped and searched? As for the proscription of a number of organisations, how would the difference between active and passive support be considered? Those who guarded our security could hardly avoid relying on their own perceptions and those could be affected by latent prejudice or intuitive 'hunch'.

Anti-Terrorism Crime and Security Act 2001 (ATCSA)

Now legislation was coming along hastily in the wake of the 11 September 2001 attack on New York. The new Act, seen by some as harsher than its predecessor, was certainly more comprehensive in detail.

The chief provisions of the Act are as follows:

- Suspected terrorist assets to be seized, suspicious bank accounts frozen;
- Home Secretary allowed to identify any non-British citizen suspected of terrorist links and detain them indefinitely pending deportation, even when this might be prohibited;
- A substitution in existing criminal law of 'racially or religiously aggravated' for 'racially aggravated';
- Illegal now to deal in biological or chemical weapons. Illegal to disclose information which might prejudice the security of any nuclear site or of any nuclear material. Improved security of dangerous substances of interest to terrorists;
- New regulations for the detention of aircraft where an act of violence against anyone on board is suspected;
- Police to be allowed to forcibly obtain fingerprints and other features to assist ascertainment of identity. Ministry of

Defence police allowed to operate in civilian areas outside military bases in certain circumstances;

▪ Streamlining of immigration procedures;

▪ Home Secretary may be in contact with telephone companies and Internet providers to access and retain data for the purpose of enhancing security.

In the final stages of parliamentary discussion of the Bill, there was sharp adverse criticism. The Lord Chief Justice, Lord Woolf, told the BBC in December 2001 that he was deeply worried by aspects of the Act. 'It is important', he said, 'that the limitations are not in place any longer than is absolutely necessary.' Normal appeal procedure for suspected terrorists detained without trial was to be abolished. Were we not over-reacting to the events of 11 September? This legislation harmed the United Kingdom's reputation for upholding the rule of law; it sent out 'damaging signals'.

Criticism swelled into outrage in some quarters over powers in the Act, when published, to detain indefinitely pending possible deportation. Surely this was a step beyond the bounds of the European Convention on Human Rights, Article 5, where deportation to another country would never be permitted if torture were a possibility? The Government, now with its back to the wall, argued that there was a state of emergency threatening the life of the nation. Derogations from Article 5 were then put in hand. Inevitably, appeals against deportation were lodged and gathered valuable support. Despite widespread disbelief, the claim of a state of emergency was approved in Parliament in 2003 and 2004. Subsequently, there ensued so many legal challenges to some of the Act's provisions that the Law Lords, on 16 December 2004, ruled that detention powers in the Act of 2001 in Part 4, and applying only to foreign nationals, were indeed incompatible with UK obligations to the European Convention and the right to freedom from any discrimination. A possible derogation could not be allowed since there was not an observable state of emergency threatening national life and the powers sought were not proportionate to any terrorist threat that the United Kingdom was facing. The Law Lords further declared that the Act's provisions for detention without trial were incompatible with the Convention.

Today's opinion of the 2001 Act sees it as a tentative flexing of government muscle against much disbelief about the workability of the legislation. Lord Woolf's strictures netted wide publicity. Whitehall should think again about infringements. Part 4 powers to deal with terrorist certification, detention and deportation were at length repealed and replaced with a system of Control Orders in the Prevention of Terrorism Act 2005. Five years were to elapse before the inadequacies of 2001 were addressed by a rather abashed government still resolute in protecting and preventing in ways which could earn it a respectful following.

Striking the balance between security and liberty in the context of threats from international terrorism was never got quite right in the ATCSA. Earnest discussions went on in Whitehall in 2002 and 2003, and in 2004 the Home Secretary released a response to the Act from a cross-party committee from both parliamentary Houses. Quite firmly, the unsatisfactory Part 4 was condemned. Long-term derogation from human rights obligations surely had 'a corrosive effect on the culture of respect for human rights'. Shortcomings in the ATCSA called for replacement of Part 4. There was a chance of putting things straight with precautions against discrimination, indefinite detention and other controversial points, if a new Act were tabled for 2005.

The Prevention of Terrorism Act 2005

This time the Government had designed new proposals with three things in mind. Prime need was to work a new deal over the procedures of detention, charging, court hearings and deportation. Then, to convince the public that necessary government powers did not endanger civic rights. Furthermore, never again must a charge of 'an affront to democracy' be levelled at Whitehall lawmakers.

The chief provisions of the Act are as follows:

▪ Home Secretary allowed to issue Control Orders for people suspected of terrorist involvement;

▪ Continued indefinite detention of suspects without trial;

▪ A ban on possession of certain articles or substances likely to be useful in terrorism;

▪ Restrictions on association and communication with specified others, again, in connection with suspects;

▪ A ban on the use of the Internet or telephones by suspect terrorists;

▪ A requirement to allow officials to seize materials, enter and search homes and remove items for testing. Also, a requirement for suspects to provide on demand any information related to terrorism.

Government justifications for Control Orders were prominently reported in the press. The Orders were to be used only in a limited number of carefully selected cases and they were to be 'tailored' to the risk posed by the individual concerned. Safeguards were there to protect human rights. Where the person under control could not see evidence against them, it was for security reasons, but an appointed legal representative might do an inspection. Each Control Order had to have a mandatory review by the High Court. Finally, these Orders were stated to be a necessary and pro-portionate response to current threats.

In brief, the main provisions of Control Orders were as follows:

▪ Prohibited access to specific services such as the Internet, restrictions on named individuals and, in some cases, on movement;

- Home Secretary to apply for court permission to impose an Order in the light of assessment of intelligence information;

- Open or closed court sessions to decide individual cases depending on the nature and sensitivity of intelligence received;

- Control Orders may be imposed for 12 months at a time. Fresh renewal application will then be necessary;

- A Control Order and its conditions may be challenged;

- Breach of Order obligations is a criminal offence punishable with a prison sentence of up to five years or an unlimited fine.

To date, the UK Government has not sought an Order requiring derogation from Article 5 of the European Convention on Human Rights. If the Government had hoped to allay a furore of complaints about fresh legislation, they must have been taken aback by the gale that blew in Parliament's two Houses and in the press. At early stages of the projected Bill, commentators spoke of 'the ping-pong between both houses . . . evidence of an unusual constitutional crisis . . .' It was the new Control Orders that led to most unhappiness. The previous chapter, 'The state of play', recounted the tactical manoeuvring to get the Orders acceptable to the country as a whole. Here, we are more concerned with legal ramifications.

In early 2005 the House of Lords entered a substantial number of amendments to the Bill. There should be a 'sunset clause' so that the Act would expire automatically in March 2006 unless renewed by further legislation. Judges rather than politicians should authorise Control Orders. It would be important to restore the normal 'burden of proof' rather than the weaker 'balance of probabilities'. Amendments such as these, stressing such fundamental rights, were unacceptable to the House of Commons at first. Eventually, through clever compromises, both Houses accepted the promise of legislative review within 12 months. Even so, was the new legislation short-circuiting the ancient principle of habeas corpus? And was it really ethical and humane to put the protection of the freedom of UK citizens to go about without fear of terrorism as a higher priority than guaranteeing the civil liberties of suspected terrorists? Elected politicians, rather than judges, under a thin veneer of legality, would now effectively deprive us of our liberty. Once more, as the year 2006 dawned, minds were focused on shaping yet more anti-terrorism legislation.

Terrorism Act 2006

Some indication of the tenor of a new act had already been given by the Prime Minister, Tony Blair, in August 2005, one month after London's July bombing. He acknowledged that each tightening of the law had met with fierce opposition and defeats in Parliament. This time the Government had conducted extensive surveys of practice in other countries, in particular in Europe.

The chief provisions of the Act are as follows:

- Prohibition of materials which offer people direct or indirect encouragement or inducement to prepare, commit or instigate terrorist acts;
- Prohibition of dissemination of terrorist publications (maximum penalty prison sentence of seven years);
- Prohibition of preparation of anyone for intended terrorist acts (maximum penalty life imprisonment);
- Prohibition of any terrorist training or attendance at training places;
- Careful guarding of nuclear sites, devices, facilities and materials against illegal access or possession;
- Home Secretary given wider powers in regard to group proscription, short-term detention of suspects, searches and interception of communications.

Detention proposals led to far-flung public argumentation. In November 2005 a government amendment to the Bill called for suspects to be held for a period of 90 days. This was a considerable increase over the term permitted by Terrorism Act 2000 allowing a maximum of 14 days. Repeatedly the Government made the point of police advice that 90 days afforded more time for investigations. Opposition to 90 days was relentless. Such a head-on challenge to traditional liberties could never be justified regardless of any terrorist threat. This was a police state in the making. Democracies were not to imprison without trial for any length of time.

The House of Commons threw out the 90 day suggestion. They settled, rather, for 28 days. Some backbenchers pushed for extension to 42 days. They failed. As the Act went through the caustic view of Conor Gearty in *The Guardian* gained fair press coverage:

The 90 day, 28 day fracas is just the latest of many affronts to the rule of law, the attack on political speech, the wide administrative discretion, the vague crimes, the expansion of proscriptive power, above all, the truncated legal procedures . . . with which we fool ourselves that we remain in touch with our liberal past . . .

(There is further discussion of the detention issue later in Chapter 8.)

There is no slackening in the rate at which the Government considers the shape of projected legislation to defeat terrorism, nor is there any sign of diminished public concern and debate.

In January 2008 the Home Secretary, Jacqui Smith, gave a major counter-terrorism speech at a London conference. At the moment, she said, there were five major terrorist trials underway in UK courts. The previous year 42 people had been convicted for terrorist offences relating to 16 known operations. Half of them pleaded guilty. The terrorist threat was real and live. Terrorist outrages were crimes, first and foremost. The law sought to strengthen prosecution and to improve ways in which suspects are dealt with after they have been charged. Impending legislation, she promised, would contain the following provisions:

■ Judges to be able to impose longer sentences where terrorist connections are thought of as an 'aggravating factor';

■ Persons convicted of terrorism-related offences to be put on a special register;

■ Introduction of powers to seize the assets of convicted terrorists.

The US approach

Nobody can fail to understand or underestimate the trauma that affected the United States in September 2001. The tragedy of some 3,000 deaths in America's heartland gripped the public absolutely. Both the President and the Administration must have experienced a feeling of electrified shock and uncertainty as to what course of action to adopt.

Hayward and Morrison (2002) have discussed the symbolism of 9/11's 'Ground Zero' and the general puzzlement as to whether the attack should be considered a 'crime' or 'war'. What, then, would be the appropriate government response? As New York reeled from the incident the immediate plan was to accelerate Pentagon hauling in of suspect terrorists to the police. Courts, whether criminal or military, with their conventions about evidence and defendant rights were judged too unwieldy. President Bush, as Commander-in-Chief, appeared ready to disregard practically all accepted bounds of the law, if national security demanded it. One example of this was the system of detention and interrogation which had to be on lines laid down in Geneva in 1949; in defiance of this terrorist suspects would be tried by military commissions as in Guantanamo Bay, Cuba. Suspect terrorists would be branded 'illegal enemy combatants' whose bizarre future the President would decide.

Admittedly, in autumn 2001 most feelings were raw and aggressive. A state of 'extraordinary emergency' had been proclaimed.

White House personnel were tight-lipped and determined to lean on those 'soft on terror'. They were intent on keeping Presidential power and executive capabilities at zenith even though that was rated as 'dictatorial'.

In *The New York Times Magazine* of 9 September 2007, there is an account of how certain lawyers, at the President's elbow, were growing increasingly concerned, skirting around the Constitution as anti-terrorism provisions were pushed out for Congress approval. President Bush was facing enormous pressure to be aggressive and pre-emptive in adopting means to prevent another attack. Jack Goldsmith, key constitutional advisor to the President, soon found himself at odds with White House standpoints. He was troubled that the Bush Administration was following a 'go-it-alone' view of executive power instead of reaching out to Congress and the courts for support. Goldsmith deplored the fact that much of the legal counsel reaching the ear of President Bush came from a self-styled war council, very small and 'hawkish'. Above all, he saw in the Administration's reluctance to question maltreatment of suspects, especially to do with torture, proof of lack of care for human conventions. Might not the War Crimes Act even be used to prosecute officials for their attitude to detainees? In so many ways, Government was approaching anti-terrorism schemes with a concept of power that relied on 'minimal deliberation, unilateral action and legalistic defense'. (This charge might also have applied to much of the Blair Government approach in the United Kingdom after 2001.) No proper lawyer could put up with such a concept among his employers. Goldsmith resigned in late 2004 after a frustrating 12 months at the White House.

What sort of law?

Eight years after 9/11 it is worth reflecting on the key issue concentrating minds in Washington. What kind of law was needed to back up counter-terrorism strategies? In mid-September 2001, President Bush, with some emotion, told his countrymen, 'We are at war'. One consequence of this was that the White House secretariat, charged generally with the task of translating presidential rhetoric into plain administrative terms, had to reach for the files on the Laws of War. Directives, abstracts and proposals had to be compiled hastily for the Oval Office. The object of such a law system in time of hostilities is to minimise unnecessary suffering and to provide for the regulation of such things as basic rights for combatants and for the protection of civilians. These conflicts may be international or non-international.

Lawyers were soon putting to the Administration the impossibility of defining parties in conflict in most of the situations that are attributed to terrorist violence. In what respects are terrorist acts different from criminal action, in which case a prosecution-and-court response is necessary? Term it a war and you have an enemy (in or out of uniform) who is fought by conventional, armed means and ultimately, one hopes, defeated. Resorting to violence in many ways are rebels, insurgents, freedom fighters, extremist cells – groups and individuals. The origins of conflict, its shape, its radiated influences, its end, are all indeterminate. If the logic of motivation-opportunity-capability is relevant, then coherent anti-terrorism must examine and work on such things as root causes and popular support. In all this, the Supreme Court would have the final say but they and the legal advisors crisply delivered a final blow to any Presidential war directive. Anti-terrorism legislation must find another form.

The US terrorist laws

In the years before 2001, legislation related to any form of terrorist activity would have taken the shape of measures to do with immigration, refugees, asylum seekers and aliens. In all these cases, status, intentions and, perhaps, attitudes to the United

States needed official enquiry and certification on lines laid down in the Immigration and Nationality Act 1952, updated in 1996. Under this Act, persons need not be suspected of terrorist or hostile intent but there were provisions for interrogation, detention and removal to a receiving country.

In 1996 President Bill Clinton signed an oddly named act, the Anti-terrorism and Effective Death Penalty Act. This was designed 'to deter terrorism, provide justice for victims, provide for an effective death penalty and for other purposes'. (Despite the impressive title, this Act was not normally going to consign a terrorist to the death chamber.) Two things in the Act brought considerable public unease. It looked as though a Federal court might be restricting the habeas corpus of terrorist suspects and as though appeals had little chance. Nor did it seem quite clear by which processes Federal judges might convict a possible terrorist. Was this Act entirely constitutional in so rigorously bearing down on those arrested?

As we have noted, legislation was expedited in September 2001. On 23 September, Executive Order 13224 was to block the assets of organisations and individuals with any link to terrorism. A list of 188 such groups and individuals was there in the Order. The year 2001 was, however, notable for a titanic enterprise, the launching of the Patriot Act, an Act for 'Uniting and Strengthening America by Providing Appropriate Tools Required to Intercept and Obstruct Terrorism'. With such a splendid title no Act could be less than quite comprehensive.

Patriot Act 2001

The chief provisions of this Act are as follows:

- Proscription of any group 'seeking to influence the policy of the Government by intimidation or coercion';
- Rigorous scrutiny and seizure of funding likely to be of use to terrorists;

- Extended surveillance procedures – wire taps, interception of the Internet and emails;
- Search warrants, entry and seizure of persons or materials may be levied without warning;
- Attorney-General given authority to detain and deport non-citizens (with little or no judicial review);
- Attorney-General given authority to designate domestic groups as terrorist organisations and to deport any non-citizens who belong;
- Presidential option for issuing Executive Orders reserving the right to decide whether a military commission is appropriate for suspects' trials.

At the ceremony of signing the Act, President Bush congratulated the military, law enforcement, Homeland Security personnel and intelligence service staff who had been working night and day. The Patriot Act would give them the tools to get the job done.

When the Act was complete and approved, one broad line of thinking queried whether the Constitution's elaborate structure of checks and balances remained in place. There seemed now only one locus of power: the Executive. The electorate was being asked not so much to understand the politico-legal 'ins and outs' as just to trust Government. How would citizens ever be able to evaluate how far these Executive powers were 'required' for anti-terrorism legislation? 'America remains at war' was the White House declaration. What would that mean for civilian 'warriors'? Notwithstanding adverse opinions, the general feeling among Americans seemed to be that of a very cautious acceptance and a hope that something more liberal in the way of anti-terrorism legislation would emerge. Few lawyers were of this mind.

A recent attempt to consolidate anti-terrorism law is the Intelligence Reform and Terrorism Protection Act 2004. This move, most think, was to reassure both lawyers and an increasingly dubious public. The Government's leading rationale was that the accumulation of intelligence is the weakest link in anti-terrorism legislation. Terrorist attack was most likely to take place within the domestic area. Correspondingly, it was 'domestic intelligence that must be sharpened'. The surveillance of the FBI had been 'lackluster', in the words of the Act. Their case-by-case working methods did not suit counter-terrorism operations. Modern surveillance is very much 'high-tech'. Modern terrorist countering (backed by an appropriate law) is not case-oriented and is freewheeling with an experimental edge. Intelligence systems must be remade. A point stressed in the Act is that when intelligence agencies operate 'at home', rather than abroad, a number of civil liberties and fundamental rights have to be observed. Remaking must provide for remembering the vital need to acknowledge and confirm the place of basic human rights in our efforts to build public security.

The United States and the United Kingdom have cautiously moved along similar trajectories in an attempt to remodel and modernise the essentials of anti-terrorism legislation. We shall see in Chapter 5 that the EU has taken in hand its own legislation.

5

Laws and terrorism:
the European Union

The more we are together

Since the 1970s several things have served to concentrate political minds in Europe generally and in the EU in particular. Terrorist activity has spread within Europe itself, as well as in the Middle East and South-east Asia. The Soviet invasion of Afghanistan, the Islamic revolution in Iran and the problems of Iraq-at-war have brought home to European states their growing impotence on the international scene when confronted by anti-Western hostility. Common responses are generally to be indisputable, concerted, appropriate and legitimate. As the years have rolled by, an increasing amount of interstate teamwork has gone into thinking out and putting into effect agreed schemes. To take counter-terrorist polices as an example, movement has been in two directions: (a) strategic and tactical and (b) legal. There has been notable progress in the first area in pooling ideas, marshalling resources and girding up for restorative action. At first sight, the objectives and means to realise them, which are set out in Europe's Action Plan of 2002: The State of Play and in the EU Counter-terrorism Strategy of 2005, have all needed and secured authenticity and legitimacy. This, though, is the machinery to get to grips with terrorists, on the ground, as it were. It is the second direction that has presented the most problems. The strategies and the tactics must be backed up legally. Progress there has been frustratingly slow.

Normally, in the past, these threats have been dealt with by foreign offices and by civil law, when the problems were discernible and likely to explode. The last two decades have seen an expansion of irregular, often unpredictable, violence which is difficult to control and almost impossible to reduce with the conventional tools of detection, charge, detention and judicial hearing. Europe, in the shape of the EU, is a collection of nation states with rights and obligations and an obvious requirement for protected security and constitutional rules. Customary practice in meeting a threat has been for each nation to reassert its authority and to devise measures judged appropriate to meet the challenge. This will no longer suffice, given the nature of international terrorist activities. As earlier chapters have recounted, Europe's Member States have banded together to counter terrorism with carefully thought out strategies and tactics and resolutely put them into joint action.

Lawyers in Europe are able to demonstrate faith in harmonising approaches to security. Shortly after the Second World War, the legal foundations of working for peace were laid down as the European Defence Community (1953). A Solemn Declaration on European Unity followed in 1983, with stress there on the obligations Members must observe to maintain the unity. Ten years later, the Amsterdam Treaty put before Europe the three-fold, interrelated goals of freedom, security and justice with, once again, a strong emphasis on Members' responsibility to achieve those goals. As far back as 1977, Europeans were aware of increasing political extremism, particularly in Spain and Northern Ireland, and came together to design and promulgate the European Convention on the Suppression of Terrorism.

Present-day readers may wonder why, in view of the impressive rhetoric of the EU, the actual legal arrangements to undergird counter-terrorism are so tardy and confused.

The position in Europe is a feature of the US State Department's comprehensive survey of terrorist activity country by country, which by law must be submitted each 30 April. The survey of April 2008 records 10 years of terrorist incidents in the United Kingdom, Spain, France, Germany, the Netherlands and Poland. Islamic militants have threatened Italy – 'after London it is Rome's turn' – and Denmark. By good fortune lately the Winter Olympics and the World Cup have remained trouble free. A study in 2007 by the Department of Comparative Politics, University of Bergen traces incidents between 1962 and 2004 and shows high activity peaks for as long as 1971 to 1990 and thereafter a continuous threat-potential in 18 European states. Europol, in 2004, concluded that there is an ongoing threat from 'a wide number of groups and organisations ranging from international Jihadist networks and large-scale Nationalist groups to violent political extremists generally involved in acts of sabotage and criminal damage'. Scenarios such as eco-terrorism, bio-terrorism, and cyber-terrorism are, according to Europol, very worrying possibilities, difficult to forestall and to deal with.

Why, in view of this, Human Rights Watch asks, are we all so slow in using the law as a potent counter-terrorism weapon? In any case, it affirms, present and proposed security measures must be in full conformity with international human rights law, international humanitarian law and international refugee protection standards. If only justice ministries were not so reverential towards classic definitions of sovereignty and autonomy, many people say. If only they were less jealous of their own manufactured prerogatives. If only they could display more tolerance and respect towards lawmakers in other lands. Would it be so difficult to match minds and resolution in agreeing on definitions and ways of working towards practicable solutions? Yet again, with the threat at everybody's front door, is not the immediacy and the scale of the terrorist challenge enough to push states' lawyers into working for legal 'approximation'? That is the term and the objective the EU would like to see realised. In truth, realisation as an end in itself does tend to divide those impatiently calling for decisive action – numerous members of European legislatures, police and security personnel – and many lawyers and government officials concerned about priorities, precedent and customary rules.

Definition

European nations working together with the aims of decision and action need to have in mind a clear understanding of the meaning of 'terrorism'. Definition has been given priority despite difficulties and inevitable controversies. All legal approaches in countering terrorism depend upon consensus as to its meaning.

Recognising the convergence of states' interests, the Council of Europe in 1977 fashioned a European Convention on the Suppression of Terrorism. There was no comprehensive definition in it, rather, a listing of terrorist acts defined either autonomously or with reference to international conventions. This was a kind of definition by the back door since states would have to go to existing law to investigate and prosecute. The lack of clear definition to clarify and standardise was gradually becoming plain.

As in so many respects the outrage of 9/11 concentrated minds. The European Parliament called for a unified search for legal meanings and within 10 days the Council of Europe set to work. Nine months later, in June 2002, the Framework on Countering Terrorism was adopted by the Council and all its members. The aim was to provide a uniform legal framework as a foundation for securing terrorist acts. It was commonly accepted as a definition of terrorist offences, as well as rules of state competence and ways of legal cooperation between the EU Member States. The definition (actually accepted after much argument) put terrorism as a criminal offence against persons and property:

(which) may seriously damage a country or an international organisation where committed with the aim of: seriously intimidating a population; or unduly compelling a government or international organisation to perform or abstain from performing any act; or seriously destabilising or destroying the fundamental, political, constitutional, economic or social structures of a country or an international organisation.

This is not the crispest of the hundred or so definitions in common currency. As might be expected it is concerned with action against states and sub-state interests rather than with the all too frequent militancy and violence directed to terrifying and injuring individual citizens. Nevertheless, firm legal standpoints are established. An innovation was the distinction between three types of terrorist offence, not so obvious perhaps in the definition above as in the Framework details that fill out the definition. There are violent terrorist acts, there is the violence in association of a terrorist group and there is the criminality of terrorist supporters. States could activate legal procedures by referring to their own domestic laws when they themselves were directly threatened. There were also rules to deal with cases where an offence falls within the jurisdiction of more than one Member State.

Press comment appraising Europe's anti-terrorism efforts has been rather thin and infrequent. A fair example of informed reporting is to be found in the US *International Herald Tribune* of 18 April 2007. Inter-government collaboration is seen as reasonable, given the odds against it and the obvious difficulty of working with 27 differing law systems. Complex and problematical areas remain. Collaboration over the European Arrest Warrant, definition of terrorism, comparison of charge and court procedures and of subsequent punishment nature and routine have all moved more effectively than was anticipated. Progress, too, is visible in bringing together the different functional and territorial roles of national police forces. Yet, the paper affirms, the old preference for each nation coping legally with a threat to their own security is a resolve putting brakes on EU rationalisation. And everybody knows that the majority of lawyers seldom strike out for the radical rather than the long-held conventions.

The legal Framework was intended to 'harmonise relevant criminal law and jurisdictional rules reflecting the agreement of Member States on central terrorist issues'. Basic to this objective was the alignment of the states' legislation along the following lines:

- Agreement on definition of terrorist offences (individual or group);

- Offences to be punishable in all Member States by 'effective, proportionate and dissuasive criminal penalties, which may entail extradition';

- Provision should be made for 'mitigating circumstances' (e.g. 'collaboration with police and judicial authorities, finding evidence or identifying the other offenders');

- An agreement on means of protection of victims and their appropriate assistance.

Later refinements in 2004 and 2005 to the first outlining of states' responsibilities stressed again an information exchange (while respecting the fundamental right to data protection) and the bringing together of 'law enforcement agencies' across all 27 Member States.

The hoped-for legal rationalisation in Europe seems to have proceeded smoothly, save that rather slow progress was to be expected with transposition, that is, the incorporation of agreed measures into Members' national laws, across the language divide. Rights to defence and to fair trial, very much the bedrock of law, have had to be 'translated', most carefully. From time to time there have been amendments to the Framework of 2002. Member States have been keen to harmonise their approaches to terrorist provocation, incitement, propaganda dissemination and recruitment and training, all factors in radicalisation and recruitment not altogether covered by existing national laws. These forms of behaviour are now to be punishable whether committed directly between persons or indirectly through the Internet. The focus on direct and indirect associations with terrorism is especially important in the attempt, by means of plain definition, to narrow down and regularise what was formerly too wide an array of what were considered to be terrorist offences. There was always the danger that people engaged in legitimate political or social dissent might be branded as terrorists. Tightening up legality was an urgent job to be done.

Stepping stones to unity

The Amsterdam Treaty took six years of drafting before its final shaping in 1997, an illustration of problems in bridging quagmires. We have noted the triple goals of freedom, security and justice. The Treaty compilers in Brussels were well aware of how closely and traditionally Member States guarded responsibility for security within their own discrete frontiers. Thus, in the Treaty's innovative design for a Common Foreign and Security Policy (CFSP) Brussels must have been prepared to anticipate at least a degree of measured caution in European foreign offices. Tactfully, it must have been put to diplomats, that in the fact of terrorism, 'there can be no other way'. It is probably true that those who urged consensus, and were providing the means for it, were also ready to grant some compromise, some latitude, if all were to come on board. Hence, Amsterdam put in a clause permitting 'constructive abstention', a clever diplomatic device allowing a Member State to take up a 'reserved position' in approving a group decision without blocking it.

Compromise is to be found in the Convention on the Suppression of Terrorism of 1977 and it is worth looking at in some detail. Meeting in Strasbourg in January 1977 a number of EU Member States agreed not to extradite anyone indicted for a political offence. The compromise here was in taking account of the positions of Norway, Sweden and Switzerland, long proud of their reputation for offering asylum to political refugees.

Unhesitatingly, these states were committed to take effective action against terrorism and common criminals and they recognised that extradition could remove terrorists. They were never prepared to extradite political offenders. This group decision seems at odds with the common view that most terrorists are politically motivated. The decision rankled in some quarters where there was surprise that the EU was disregarding 'loopholes'. At length, state representatives came together once more in 1996 and this time rescinded the earlier agreement. Political association and motivation would be used no longer as reasons for refusing extradition. All were of the view now that extradition would materially help the process of getting rid of identified terrorists.

One more example of compromise by way of inducement may be noted in the consequences of the Schengen Acquis (Agreement) 1995. When this came into effect in the EU, it abolished checks at the borders of signatory states and created a single external border where immigration checks for the Schengen area are carried out in accordance with identical procedures. (The United Kingdom did not join the Acquis, doubtless feeling that its security was controllable on its side of the English Channel.) Common rules concerning visas, rights of asylum and checks at external borders were adopted to allow the free movement of persons within the signatory states without disrupting law and order.

In order to reconcile freedom and security, this freedom of movement was accompanied by so-called 'compensatory measures'. This involved improving cooperation and coordination between the police and judicial authorities in order to safeguard security and the tackling of organised crime. With this in mind, the Schengen Information Service (SIS) was set up. SIS is a sophisticated database used by the authorities of the Schengen Member Countries to track and exchange data on certain categories of people and goods and to identify terrorist suspects. Doubts were not altogether dispelled. Germany's Interior Minister and police warned apprehensively of a possible 'criminal wave' taking advantage of their loosened borders. In France, the Sureté lost no time in installing an ambitious anti-terrorist surveillance system.

An agenda for united action-in-law

The Amsterdam Treaty launched an agenda which Members of the EU should follow in seeing to security coordination. Recently, the European Commission has described procedures in detail:

Actions have been developed in four directions regarding judicial cooperation in criminal matters. First, EU Member States have agreed to approximate the definition of offences and the level of sanctions for certain types of offences when they had transnational aspects. Second, just as mutual recognition of national standards was essential in achieving the European single market, mutual recognition of decisions taken by national judges is set to become the cornerstone of judicial cooperation in criminal matters. Various specific tools to facilitate practical judicial cooperation have also been adopted and are now effective.

The creation of a common area of freedom, security and justice has been asserted as an aim of the EU since the Amsterdam Treaty. As regards criminal justice, the aim is to ensure that cross-border crimes are dealt with more efficiently and that individuals have their rights guaranteed equally, no matter under which Member State's jurisdiction their case is being heard, whether they are suspects, accused or victims.

Legal approximation, coordination of proceedings, mutual recognition of final decisions and strengthening mutual confidence are the major ways to strengthen judicial cooperation in the EU. Before the adoption of the Amsterdam Treaty some work had been achieved under the Single European Act and the Maastricht Treaty in order to improve judicial cooperation in criminal matters. Conventions had been adopted, for instance, on extradition but did not enter into force because some Member States failed to ratify them. The Amsterdam Treaty provides for new legal instruments which are legally binding for Member States this substantially helped to improve the efficiency of the European Action in this field.

In October 1999, the Council of Europe held a special meeting in Tampere (Finland) which, for the first time, was exclusively devoted to issues of justice and home affairs. Since the European Council of Tampere, EU activities in the field of criminal justice have been developed in four directions:

- Approximation of legislation;
- Development of interests based on the mutual recognition principle;
- Improvement of judicial cooperation mechanisms;
- Development of relationships with foreign countries.

Reinforcement of EU legal action

Counter-terrorism legislation throughout Europe, with so many states participating, clearly needs some sort of monitoring and coordinating body. At the Tampere meeting in 1999, a number of Members, Germany, Portugal, France and Sweden, pressed for the establishment of such an agency, ideally with its office in The Hague. A group decision in December 2001 named the agency Eurojust and approved locating headquarters in The Hague. Each Member State must appoint a national representative to Eurojust – a prosecutor, judge or police officer (with legal credentials). These national representatives must be subject to the national law of the state that appointed them. Joint investigation, prosecuting and data-processing teams can be put together inside Eurojust from the representatives. They are to have privileged contact with EU office holders. Since the remit is pan-European policy law, confidentiality and professional liaison are most important. In every sense, Eurojust is a reinforcement to shaping the EU anti-terrorism drive.

Another reinforcement agency is the European Judicial Network (EJN) which saw daylight in 2000 after some years of exploratory discussion. With its office in Brussels, EJN aims to provide training programmes for members of the judiciary in Europe. There is a website where legal professionals can search for and exchange information. Every Member State is to appoint a legal advisor as a 'contact point' with other Members. The contacts have already adopted the logo 'Go For It' and see their role as 'active inter-mediaries' who consult, inform and train the anti-terrorism lawmakers of Europe.

Apart from continued talking and reassessment in Brussels, The Hague and most European capitals in the offices of government and lawyers, there has been straight comment from such as the International Commission of Jurists and the renowned Eminent Jurists Panel. They have taken evidence for the EU and from various governments, from NGOs, leading lawyers and academics. These organisations have put their fingers on a number of dubious practices amounting, it is inferred, to duplicity. Why do some Member States facilitate detention incommunicado and without charge and customary safeguards? Do not certain states realise the alienating effect of anti-terrorism legislation on minority communities, especially Muslims, who bear the brunt of security service powers applied indiscriminately? EU Member States too frequently are securing information through proscribed interrogation methods. Why do they not insist on their intelligence services being fully accountable? Democratic and diplomatic assurances and the basic requirements of human rights must be more fully observed. There are too many evasions and contradictions at present in much of the anti-terrorism legislation.

The anti-terrorism laws of some European states

An account of EU attempts to coordinate and 'approximate' anti-terrorism legislation can usefully conclude with a brief survey of the law in practice in a number of the EU states. In October 2005 the UK Foreign and Commonwealth Office (FCO) published a most informative survey of 'counter-terrorism legislation and practice' in ten selected countries, eight of them in Europe. The survey described the situation in mid-2005 and plans for further measures are envisaged in some capitals. The US State Department survey of April 2008 goes further over much the same ground.

France

Central to legislation here is the French Constitution of 1958 which refers explicitly to the Declaration of the Rights of Man and of the Citizen of 1789. This emphasis perhaps reflects misgivings about the drastic penal laws passed at the end of the nineteenth century to conform violent, illegal radicalism. Those *lois scélérates* refer to the harsh and unjust cutting down of French elemental freedoms. Modern France must never act like that again; in any case the state operates a dualist law system where the EU's integrated laws require domestic legislation to give it effect.

Twenty years ago Paris recruited a caucus of examining magistrates specialising in cases of terrorism. Their experimental work in investigation and prosecution was so successful that it led to the formation of a corps of anti-terrorism magistrates. The French see terrorists as a particular species of common criminal, and law bears down heavily on conspiracy, propaganda transmission, money laundering and membership of proscribed organisations. Pre-trial detention is limited to 48 hours with the possibility of 2 extensions each of 24 hours. Moreover, the French are keen not to exceed these periods and concerned not to expel or extradite French or non-French citizens without rigorous examination.

Germany

Fundamental rights in the *Grundgesetz* (Basic Law), like the inviolability of human dignity, cannot be changed even by constitutional amendment. New laws and their application are reviewed by the Federal Constitutional Court for their constitutionality. Legal definition of terrorism is less specific than is the case in France. Existing laws are considered to provide sufficient coverage. However, with the new year of 2002, an omnibus package of amendments to pre-existing statutes came into force as the Law on Fighting Terrorism.

Germany is scrupulous not to detain suspects beyond 48 hours, although 24 hours is usual. A judge needs to be satisfied that evidence warrants a suspect's detention. There is care not to breech fundamental rights, especially of privacy, in offering admissible evidence for trial. Criticism, though, maintains that governmental banning of association with certain groups is too sweeping and the right of appeal inadequate. Nor is there satisfaction always about the grounds on which expulsion and deportation of foreigners may be ordered. Is 'hate preaching' a credible offence leading to expulsion?

Italy

In common with Germany, Italy's law is rooted in a post-Second World War constitution, that of 1948. Also, once more, a Constitutional Court scrutinises new laws. Various anti-terrorism laws were passed in the 1970s introducing something unfamiliar to Europeans, namely, spontaneity in police search and arrest without a judge's mandate. The Italian definition of terrorism is more detailed than that of most other states in Europe. Preventive detention is limited to 48 hours and, as in Germany, a judge must be satisfied about procedures for investigation, charging and detention being carried out properly.

The Italian Government has put much thought into reasons for expulsion of foreign nationals. One of the grounds for expulsion is when there is information showing that an individual is a threat to national security but evidence is insufficient for prosecution. In addition, expulsion and extradition may be ordered where a person habitually engages in criminal activity, lives wholly or in part on the proceeds of crime, behaves in a way that offends or puts at risk the moral or physical well-being of youth, public health and peace or belongs to a mafia type of organisation. No state can be more comprehensive than that!

Spain

Spaniards have never felt quite the same about any sort of terrorist violence since the Madrid bombing of 11 March 2004. Yet, they have had to deal with the violence of the Basque separatists' ETA for many anguished years. Many in Spain believe that the Government's harsh forays against the rebels have denuded the rights and daily living of other citizens. They would be inclined to add that since the Franco era democratic progress has been tardy, with only a slow lessening of repression in legislation and a gradual easing up in police operational procedures. Spain has not been affected much by external extremists until comparatively recently and the instigation from outside of the Madrid railway station bombing shocked the nation. There was possibly a trace of complacency in Government announcements and debate in the parliament, the Cortes, for it must have been assumed that legislation to deal with activities 'prejudicial to public order' was tight enough. Spain, in fact, does not have specific anti-terrorism laws. Terrorism has been treated as an aggravated form of crime. Much discussion is taking place (as it is in much of Europe) about the difficulties of legislating against 'conspiracy' and 'incitement' which now is related not so much to separatist action as to links with external terrorist organisations like al-Qaida.

In one important respect Spain differs from other European Member States: the legal system is monist not dualist. This means that ratified international treaties shall be straightforwardly incorporated into the internal legal system without extra writing up for the domestic law system. Notable, too, is the constitutional requirement since 1978 that Spain's fundamental rights and liberties 'shall be construed in conformity with the Universal Declaration of Human Rights'.

There seems a less liberal approach in the laws to do with detention and extradition. In terrorist cases, a judge may order that suspects be held incommunicado if there is reason to believe that knowledge of the detention would prejudice investigation. This is perhaps a bold affront to rights, many think, especially when no suspect is able to consult a lawyer of his/her choice. Similarly, elemental rights may easily be short changed where Spain orders extradition and goes for the 'fast-track' procedure rather than the 'ordinary'. The only means of suspending a fast-track order is to claim asylum and experience here is that the asylum authorities are only too ready to refuse consideration if they suspect the application was only a delaying tactic. At least there is the guarantee that nobody shall be extradited to a land where torture or the death penalty is a possibility. Once more we have the problem of accurately identifying potential terrorists.

Sweden

This is a dualist legal system needing fresh domestic legislation to give effect to international treaties. The Swedish Constitution requires that all domestic law be in conformity with the European Convention on Human Rights. Definition of terrorism is similar to that of other states, save that if it is not possible to prove specific intent then the case shall be dealt with under the Penal Code's regular criminal law.

We have noted earlier that Scandinavian countries hold to their tradition of readiness to offer asylum in politically related cases and Sweden is very wary about extradition procedures and has in place a high regard to preservation of fundamental human rights.

No law shall abort those rights, although, as one might expect, the liberal state has to think very hard about treatment of, say, a suspect car-bomber. There is certainly no trace of the repressive police work, the harsh detention regimes and the hastiness of court procedures seen in other parts of the EU.

Norway

In some respect Norwegian law is a little sterner than that of neighbouring Sweden. Penalties for convicted terrorists are severe although the definition of terrorism may strike some as rather ambivalent and not always clear. Norway has concentrated much police work on surveillance and sustained investigation. Liberal traditions will not stand for detention beyond 48 hours with the proviso that a judge may authorise brief extensions for further interviewing. Interrogation methods which are neglectful of basic rights are not to be tolerated. Appeal procedures are uniformly clear. Once again, a Scandinavian country is most careful to operate a scrupulously fair extradition and asylum policy.

Greece

This country has lost no time in squaring up to the scourge of terrorism facing the EU. The law cites 22 types of offence considered as terrorist acts. Acts that aim at establishing a democratic regime or at defending or restoring it, as well as acts committed in the exercise of fundamental civil, political or any other rights provided for by the Constitution of the European Convention on Human Rights are deemed not to be terrorist acts.

Greek law confers a wide-ranging assembly of powers on the security authorities to deal with those whose intentions, complicity or associations give rise to doubt. There is to be protection for witnesses and for measures of leniency for criminals, including terrorists, who cooperate with the security service. Anti-terrorism legislation in Greece does not have the careful detail one comes across in France and Germany nor is it handled by specialists in that area of the law. It is democratic and broadly acceptable to most Greeks without too much anxiety over repressive approaches and methods.

Afterthought

In May 2005, Amnesty International published a 40-page report: *Human Rights Dissolving at the Borders: Counter Terrorism and EU Criminal Law*. It is a most comprehensive account of thinking, policies and subsequent legal enactment. A feature of the report is its stress on what are considered to be fundamental issues or shortcomings. Judging from what one reads and hears said, especially in legal circles, these shortcomings are thought evident and their consequences fully deserving of careful debate. They are:

- Failure to agree on a precise definition of terrorism as a basis for framing EU laws. Vaguely worded laws are inadequate and many even, in their looseness, imperil non-violent dissenters;

- Lack of judicial review. Is there no role here for the European Court of Justice? Without a systematic review system, terrorist suspects have little redress to challenge the validity of their designation or inclusion on a list;

- Lack of insistence that Member States' extradition requests are only granted when human rights in the second country are fully protected.

Amnesty feels strongly that it is time for a comprehensive review of anti-terrorism legislation in the EU, on both an EU-wide and a national basis. Should the European Commission attempt this? Or the projected EU Agency for Human Rights?

It seems to be clear, in Amnesty's words, that 'it is in the breach, not in the respect of human rights, that security is threatened'.

6

Counter-terrorism tactics and rights: United Kingdom and United States

The United Kingdom

Guardians one might term them. They are the United Kingdom's chief official security bodies – the Home Office, MI5 and the Metropolitan Police Service. There is, in fact, a finely organised network of security bodies working closely in association but these three bodies lead the field. Working together as they do, they continue to have separate and distinctive ways of working. The Home Office and the police both work closely with the public. In the shadow is MI5. As one might expect, all declare that they do not neglect the observance of human rights.

The Home Office

The Home Office's traditional responsibility for helping to make the United Kingdom a safe place and an environment with less crime has expanded enormously as it is pitched against the terrorist. Of prime concern is reduction of risk to the public and to the national infrastructure. Since 2003 the Home Office has had in place a long-term strategy of counter-terrorism known as CONTEST.

There are four key elements: Prevention, Protection, Pursuit, and Preparation. In every way the '4Ps' depend upon the informed, decisive collaboration of 'stakeholders', namely government departments, the emergency services, NGOs and voluntary associations, the business sector and contact with other governments where judged appropriate and feasible. The scheme runs on the following lines:

Prevention

▪ Tackling radicalisation which sustains terrorism via addressing wherever and whenever possible contributory factors such as disadvantage and discrimination;

▪ Deterring those who facilitate terrorism by challenging ideologies that justify the use of violence;

▪ Surveillance, detection, follow-up, prediction – the classic anticipatory and control methods used by police.

Protection

▪ Reducing vulnerabilities through careful, continuous oversight of crowded public places, protection of transport and key utilities, strengthening our border security;

▪ Affording appropriate security measures to specific groups and individuals. Attention to possible target people, facilities and places.

Pursuit

▪ Gathering intelligence to improve ability to identify and understand terrorist threats;

▪ Stress on collaboration to strengthen intelligence and lead to disruption of terrorists and their sponsors;.

▪ Curbing terrorist activity and bringing violators to justice.

Preparation

▪ Ensuring the United Kingdom is as ready as it can be to meet the consequences of terrorist attack by identifying potential risks, assessing the likely impact of attacks and building up capabilities for response, testing and evaluating preparedness.

- All the above preventive measures depend for thoroughness and success on public understanding and support and on collaboration with 'stakeholders'.

In addition to these operational drives, two key activities are central to the strategy:

- Targeting terrorist funding which underpins conspiracy, recruitment and training. Funds likely to have been raised for terrorism need careful identification, freezing and seizure. Again, close working with financial and business interests and law enforcement agencies is vital;

- Cooperation with the police to identify terrorist suspects and to hold them pending investigation, charging and court action. It is possible to deport those whose presence in the United Kingdom is judged 'not conductive to the public good'.

The Government, naturally, approves the nature and extent of this strategy. It has, however, come in for a good deal of criticism from civil liberties groups, such as Liberty and Amnesty International, and the press from time to time. Questions are many. Cannot terrorists be confronted and fought without sacrificing some of our human rights? Are we in any way safer when protest and non-violent attitudes and behaviour are criminalised? Is this strategy a forerunner of possible further sweeping restrictions?

Surveillance in practice

Almost certainly, the Home Office pays close attention to possible public anxieties and reservation, above all in the matter of surveillance. As far as one can make out, Whitehall is stressing several safeguards. First of all, on its website there is an outline of the regulation of surveillance methods. The Regulation of Investigatory Powers Act (RIPS) 2000 deals with methods of information gathering to help in the prevention of crime, including terrorism. Legislative detail complies with the Human Rights Act 1998. Provision is made for the interception of communications, the acquisition and disclosure of accumulated data, the use of surveillance techniques, the employment of covert investigators and informers and means of access to electronic data. Second, those using such methods must keep in mind the criteria of necessity and proportionality. Authorities granting permission for usage must believe that surveillance is vital to the successful outcome of a particular case. Also, any tactics intruding upon privacy must be proportionate to desired solutions which may not have been obtained reasonably by other means.

The increasing use of CCTV in security coverage has resulted in much public unease. UK society now employs an estimated 4.2 million cameras in parks, pedestrianised streets, residential neighbourhoods and transport interchanges – 1 for every 14 people. Thought of by authority as a panacea for crime, disorder and violence the installation of public 'bugging' devices arouses public concern and suspicion. In 2007 a survey carried out by Strathclyde Police in Scotland found seven out of ten in the street fearing covert watching. Generally, passers-by question barriers to their right to anonymity in public places and impediments to their right to personal movement, association, communication and response. It is difficult to obtain precise statistics of such interference beyond the numbers of those subjected to further interference via search-and-arrest. (See Chapter 8.)

Of all the counter-terrorism tactics, it is interception which has earned most brickbats and questioning. In days when communication devices were less sophisticated than they are now, the law permitted interception of communications by law enforcement agencies and the security services in tightly controlled circumstances and only in the interests of national security and the prevention and detection of serious crime. Codes of Practice were used to offset improper use. Interception is now resorted to much more frequently than hitherto, and the number of people wanting to intercept has increased exponentially. This conjunction worries many, both in and out of officialdom. On 6 February 2008 *The Guardian* put it that some 800 public bodies can now request permission to 'scoop and snoop'. Every police force in the land and 474 local authorities can 'bug' mobile and landline telephone calls, postal correspondence and emails. Security services may listen in to terrorists' talk, and a great deal of non-terrorist personal data is becoming accessible. Critics, deploring this openness, reckon with a state of paranoia justified only by that catchall term 'the war on terror'. They remind us that in 2007 Prime Minister Tony Blair said, '9/11 changes everything'. We were into 'a different game'.

The Home Office continues to innovate and develop counter-terrorism strategies and tactics. A National Counter-terrorism Security Office in partnership with the Security Service spearheads support of the Home Office's CONTEST strategy, particularly the Protect and Prepare strands of the strategy. Specialist staff can offer advice about public security measures. The office also trains, tasks and coordinates a nationwide network of centrally funded, specialist police advisors. These Counter-terrorism Security Advisors, some 136 in number, have the responsibility of aiding local police forces to assess the degree of risk to local critical sites that might be vulnerable to terrorist attack. A crucial job is to develop security awareness and readiness through relationships with professional and trade associations and various community groups.

In February 2007 major changes, by way of a 'shake-up', were announced in Whitehall. Within hours the Home Office and the new Office of Security and Counter-terrorism were to be responsible for a UK-wide counter-terrorism strategy, and their business would be reported and discussed regularly at 10 Downing Street under the chairmanship of the Prime Minister. Useful in some eyes, the reorganisation did not please everybody, with MI5 worried that it might lose some of its autonomy.

There was rather more support in Parliament for a newly constituted Ministry of Justice taking on the legal aspects of countering-terrorists.

Once more we have to credit Government with some watchfulness over public reaction. Stressing that interception is an important tool in the United Kingdom's fight against terrorism and organised crime, Whitehall is not convinced that the benefits of changing the law on interception outweigh the risks of doing so. A modest increase in convictions might be achieved, although modern criminals can change communications if they are aware of interception. Nevertheless, the Home Office is working on legal models for evidential interception that should not reveal sensitive working methods, capabilities and techniques underpinning effective counter-terrorism. They must keep in mind the fact that evidence obtained through interception is not presently admissible in any English court.

MI5

Many regard this organisation with a sniff of apprehension. Reservations about a cloak-and-dagger unit may have been in the thoughts of Members of Parliament told in July 2006 that MI5 was to be brought out into the open now. At the same time the House was told that the remit of MI5 operations had much in common with the Home Office strategy and the '4Ps'. This announcement was intended to reassure parliamentary observers that fundamental rights of citizens were not in danger. Could we be sure that there would be no dirty-tricks campaigning? The wide role of MI5 spans protection of democratic and economic interests against threats and subversion through activity in counter-terrorism, counter-intelligence and counter-espionage. The intelligence work moves through detection, surveillance, interrogation, arrangements for detention and liaison with the Prison Service. It is an investigation and protection agency without its own police powers.

The business of counter-terrorism was in the hands of MI5's Joint Terrorism Analysis Centre (JTAC), formed as the UK centre for assessment of international terrorism. Representatives of 16 government departments and the police feed their expertise into JTAC. How this Centre operates is explained on an open-to-all MI5 website. Primarily, the role is that of intelligence-gathering collation and evaluation of data. This 'raw intelligence' is processed into counter-action terms. Preventive responses can then be planned and authorised. Investigation of questionable individuals builds personality profiles and yields clues to intentions, plans and capabilities. As with the Home Office, necessity and proportionality are key requirements. Care must be taken to legitimise approaches to persons and to avoid 'collateral intrusions' against individuals other than the target. It is certainly interesting and commendable that a covert, separate agency now takes pains to spell out aims and objectives for public Internet browsers. Most critics of this silent service acknowledge that not too much may be divulged about 'finding the right blend of techniques to meet the requirements of an investigation'. Silence and secrecy may irritate those who hold the free exercise of human rights sacred but MI5 has not only to avoid compromising running investigations but also to protect the secrecy of methods so that they can be used in the future. Perhaps inevitable, also, is the prospect that the exigencies of coping with some terrorist incident will mean 'first [operational] things first'.

It is worth noting that responsible opinion in the United States, largely on Capitol Hill, thinks well of MI5. In their view the UK agency does have close regard for an individual's rights and freedoms, even though the country does not have a written constitution. MI5's investigative procedures are not cluttered up with the legal niceties that the FBI has to take account of. Legal and operational work is coordinated but kept separate. It could be said at this point, though, that lawyers in both the United States and United Kingdom worry about that separation as possibly keeping the law away from ongoing tactics. Surveillance and 'data-mining' invade the privacy of thousands of people on the off-chance of finding a few rotten apples.

The Metropolitan Police Service

A third set of Guardians, centred on London, is the Metropolitan Police Service. No longer the Bobby on the Beat, the force is highly specialised and experienced. The Anti-terrorist Branch (so termed) and a Special Branch have been dealing with an unprecedented number of counter-terrorist enquiries within the United Kingdom and, by extension, in Europe since 2000. Then, in July 2005, the terrorist attacks on London's transport links, which took 52 lives, thrust into prominence the drastic, complex, scarcely predictable elements of what a terrorist can do. There seemed to be a need for fresh thinking, new structures and more sophisticated approaches to public security. Special Branch was busy with its own ways of gathering intelligence, as well as the armed, personal protection of government officials menaced by terrorists and assisting other government agencies with security threats. A Counter-terrorist Command took over in October 2006. Expert teams with new methods would be able to respond quickly to any type of investigation or incident. As they put it, 'conference' with the public enhanced what they might do operationally. Local communities could put specific considerations to their Guardians. Working together in this fashion, police and public would be able to counter terrorism through a shared London Resilience Plan. Rather more obviously than with other Guardians, the policeman and his street-wise ally would work together not only for containment but also for justice.

The SUS procedures

A counter-terrorist tactic frequently leading to vigorous argument is the 'stop and undertake search' routine more familiar as the 'SUS procedure'. Originating as a conventional police method, not very often employed, it is now a familiar and frequent form of quasi-predictive control exercised in London streets. It is quite often referred to in the newspapers and is a much talked over element in the 'Together Against Terror' conferences the Metropolitan Police Service arranges now and then in the boroughs of the capital. Community engagement against possible threat is said to depend upon face-to-face encounter, with trust on both sides. 'Why, then, do those in Big Boots stop us so often and abruptly?' is the question from black people and Asians. 'If the policeman has to look further into his "reasonable suspicion" of an offence having been committed or about to be committed, why is it us two times out of three?' is the next question. Yes, there is discomfort, attempts at avoidance, often a failure to understand language and poise, but why is it 'us' singled out so much? Questions such as these are the ones police and public workshops try to answer and clarify.

Liberty, speaking up for rights observance, has published clear and helpful guidelines as to SUS powers and their uses. By parliamentary act, the police have the authority to enter premises, with a warrant, to deal with or prevent a breach of the peace or to save a life or limb. Again, necessity and proportionality rule as to whether rights laid down in the Human Rights Act 2000 and the European Convention on Human Rights will be fully or partially observed. On its website Liberty has the following to say about SUS and human rights:

When a police officer reasonably suspects you are a terrorist you can be stopped and searched to discover whether you have anything in your possession that could constitute evidence that you're a terrorist. Since being a terrorist is not in itself an offence (sic!), unless you are a member of a proscribed group, this power means that the police do not have to suspect you of committing an offence or of carrying prohibited articles.

In addition the police can designate specific areas to be places where they have special powers in relation to terrorism. This means that in these localities people and vehicles can be stopped and searched by the police if they consider it expedient to do so to prevent acts of terrorism. There is no need for any reasonable suspicion. They should be looking for articles which could be used in connection with terrorism but the powers can be used whether or not the police have grounds for suspecting the presence of articles of that kind.

Plainly put by a Liberty watchfulness group. Nevertheless, the quotation seems to highlight the vagueness of the term 'terrorist' and the considerable room there is for debate. The websites of the Home Office and of Liberty go into considerable detail. A summary arrest may be a consequence of SUS procedure. There are numerous powers of arrest under warrants issued by a Justice of the Peace (JP) or a judge. Statutory rules govern these. Police handling has to respect the right to liberty and personal security set out in Article 5 of the European Convention on Human Rights. Police are well aware of this. Representatives of ethnic groups are less sure. Where is the necessity and proportionality in our harassment? In our being hauled away to the local police station? Will we be questioned and then released? What do terrorists look like? Do they all have black faces? Or speak Bengali? We know our rights. And we are all absolutely against the barbarism of terrorism.

A more careful application of stop-and-search is the so-called National Security Package that the Home Office has constructed after discussion with the Metropolitan Police Service. The idea is to offer people other than police personnel – rail and airport staff, hoteliers, public events organisers – the opportunity to practise vigilance, tolerance and , if need be, careful, systematic inspection checks. Local authorities have already recruited 160 'counter-terrorism advisors'. Regional counter-terrorism units are now to put muscle into local preparedness.

What the Guardians of our security are able and authorised to do to counter-terrorism is multivariate in approach, though possibly less considerate about rights than they ought to be. Members of the security bodies are quick to stress that it is understanding, individual and general, that makes counter-terrorism effective when strategies come off the drawing board and appropriate tactics are put into operation. Alongside of this, the preservation of fundamental rights needs the sharp eyes of the observer. As for understanding among the public, Whitehall has asked the police to consider most carefully the language they use in personal encounters. They should abandon the 'aggressive rhetoric' of some counter-terrorism and above all find ways of talking, for instance, to Muslims without implying that their community is specifically to blame for terrorist activity. Putting across the idea of sharing values is so much better than alluding to a struggle for values or a confrontation of cultures. People will stop listening if they feel they are being disparaged or attacked in some fashion. It has long been in the realisation of the police officer that latent or recurring grievances, like those in evidence in multi-ethnic societies like London, can readily fuel extremism and violence.

The United States

Like the United Kingdom, the United States has three chief security Guardians entrusted with an overall, democratic responsibility for guarding the homeland. Their 'missions' are to Defend and Protect as part of a Federal strategy for combating terrorism. An Administration overview stated this directly in 2007:

America is at war with a transnational terrorist movement fueled by a radical ideology of hatred, oppression and murder. Our National Strategy for Combating Terrorism, first published in February 2003, recognizes that we are at war and that protecting and defending the Homeland, the American people, and their livelihoods remains our first and most solemn obligation.

Our strategy also recognizes that the War on Terror is a different kind of war. From the beginning it has been both a battle of arms and a battle of ideas. Not only do we fight our terrorist enemies on the battlefield, we promote freedom and human dignity as alternatives to the terrorists' perverse vision of oppression and totalitarian rule. The paradigm for combating terrorism now involves the application of all elements of our national power and influence. Not only do we employ military power, we use diplomatic, financial, intelligence and law enforcement activities to protect the Homeland. We have broken old orthodoxies that once confined our counter-terrorism efforts primarily to the criminal justice domain.

Old orthodoxies? New ways of thinking? The strategies employed and others that are foreseeable need reappraisal from time to time. In July 2002, the US House of Representatives instructed its Permanent Select Committee on Terrorism and Homeland Security to scrutinise what the security Guardians were doing. They did not mince words in their findings. Why, they asked, do almost all Federal agencies confuse their mission directives with different definitions of terrorism? The House preferred the following rendering:

Terrorism is the illegitimate, premeditated use of politically motivated violence or threat of violence by sub-national groups against persons or property with intent to coerce government by instilling fear among the populace.

The Select Committee sought to look closely at the 'missions' of the three guardian agencies – the Federal Bureau of Investigation (FBI), the Central Intelligence Agency (CIA) and the National Security Agency (NSA).

The FBI

Doubtless recoiling from Administration criticism the FBI has come into broad daylight in recent years. It speaks of itself as 'Crime Smart' on two different fronts. First, it confronts attack planning from al-Qaida core elements overseas, second, it needs to meet threats posed by self-radicalising groups and individuals who are inspired by jihadists and living in the United States. While the FBI and CIA may share similar ideologies there will be contrasts in intention and capability. Stripped now for preventive action in the War on Terror a reassertive FBI is internationalising a mammoth counter-terrorism organisation. The FBI employs over 30,000 operatives including 12,000 special agents dispersed among the public as well as others who are intelligence and cyber analysts, language experts, scientists and information technicians. The headquarters is in Washington with a network of 56 offices in Federal states and 60 overseas in US embassies. Investigative and preventive enterprise is now masterminded by a Terrorist Threat Integration Center (TTIC) and regionally by the Joint Terrorist Task Force (JTTF).

Opened in May 2003 the aim of the TTIC is to unite intelligence from a variety of sources and to help in executive, policy-making decisions. As a hub in intelligence acquisition it has unfettered access to all terrorist-threat data, from raw reports to processed analysis. At the Center analysts measure the reliability of information from interrogated suspects, study warnings from foreign law enforcement and spy agencies, assess tips from informants, examine satellite images and read transcripts of wire-tapped conversations. They are process staff and examiners, not first-data collectors. An important duty is to compile 'the daily threat matrix' sent to the Oval Office for President and Cabinet. The JTTF is a web of more than 84 units based all around the United States who together see themselves as 'a point of fusion'. In operational terms 'fusion' is the distribution of terrorist intelligence vertically from Washington and horizontally to the units across the states. Headquarters staffing comprises 57 experts from 38 agencies – law enforcement, diplomatic, intelligence, defense, public safety and homeland security. Much of their collective surmise and survey goes into attempts to identify terrorist sleeper cells. These are the sub-agency action-poles the FBI regard as a 'transformation' in its work. Known or suspected terrorism activists, worldwide, are screened and tracked by teams now numbering nearly 4,000 specialists. So-called 'Fly Teams' stand by to respond to terrorist threats anywhere. Already they have taken off to assist enquiries in Saudi Arabia, Indonesia, Pakistan, the United Kingdom and Spain. Great importance is attached to a Terrorism Financing Operations Section (TFOS) in efforts to identify and shut down illicit funds transfers. This work particularly depends upon 'strong partnerships' across a range of corporate institutions.

A revamped FBI programme bridging domestic and international terrorist threats has not escaped liberal comment and protest. In 2006 and 2007, the American Civil Liberties Union rounded on the FBI's 'lack of accountability' in much that it was undertaking:

We are witnessing serious setbacks in the protection of civil and political rights with the United States . . . A backlash against human rights in the name of national security has affected large numbers of persons in the United States and abroad.

Voices in Congress, in *The New York Times* and on local radio strongly deplore a 'rolling back' of fundamental rights and civil liberties. Why has international law been regarded so lightly? Why, indeed, has so much ground been lost in regard to habeas corpus, migrant protection and the treatment of minorities and aliens? How is it that the rights of privacy, of free expression and of peaceful assembly are endangered by many security controls? Why is it that the FBI is so neglectful of the rights of suspects, especially if they are women or racially profiled? If readers and listeners were disturbed about rights erosion they should Do Something About It through their Representatives in Washington.

Undoubtedly, comment and criticism out there in the public realm hit hard in the sequestered halls of the FBI. Doing something about it led to a series of earnest consultations between FBI executives and lawyers from the Department of Justice. What were the best ways of reconciling urgent, drastic counter-terrorism strategies with the set-in-stone provisions of the US Constitution? Their recommendations, appearing at last in July 2007, were laboured in intent and to read them is heavy going. Nevertheless, most people were satisfied as to the signs that the Administration could have humane instincts.

The key words in the published thinking are Oversight and Compliance. The scheme was to launch two offices in Washington to conduct reviews, compliance activities and training. The first one, an Oversight Section, was to be within the Department of Justice's National Security Division. The second was a proposed Office of Integrity and Compliance at the FBI. The oversight and compliance programmes run by these offices were to be at the forefront of effort to ensure that counter-terrorism operations were conducted in a manner consistent with the nation's laws, regulations and policies and the protection of the private interests and civil liberties of US citizens. For the first time, Justice Department attorneys would have a mandate to examine all aspects of FBI programmes. This was a historical innovation as the FBI Director recognised that it 'requires striking a sometimes delicate balance, and the establishment of a compliance programme mission with an unswerving commitment to the rule of law'. It was Director Robert S. Mueller who had proposed that his FBI set up an FBI Office of Integrity and Compliance which, in his words, 'would assist management at all levels to foster and maintain a culture where ethics and compliance are paramount considerations in decision making'.

Notable movement in hoisting into prominence the safeguarding of rights was clearly evident in 2007. A most earnest discussion of Rights and Counter-terrorism took place in September 2007 in the US Senate. In debate was a bill to bring in a National Security Reform Act 2007. An issue that had already been in the minds of Senators and which had been aired in press and radio was an audit carried out by the Department of Justice in March 2007. This revealed that the FBI had been using something called National Security Letters (NSL) to obtain sensitive information about businesses and individuals where there might be a suspicion of terrorist or espionage association or activity. It looked as though the US Patriot Act 2001 in approving a general expansion of counter-terrorism had given the FBI a blank cheque to obtain 'useful' information even though there was no evidence to go on and without asking for a court order. There were Senators who believed that the Patriot Act was 'flawed' legislation, created amid the panic of 9/11. The FBI had been seriously lax in operating improperly. Anyway, an earlier Congress should not have acted so hastily in giving FBI investigators broad authority and in keeping their fingers crossed that those powers would not be misused. Those powers might be security 'building blocks' in the FBI eyes. Their use, though, was an unprecedented intrusion into citizens' privacy. NSL condemnation was even a feature of prime-time television, together with frequent, searing comments about the erosion of those elementary freedoms of speech, religion, assembly, privacy and the due process of law. Thus, Senators on the whole were anxious to frame safeguards. The National Security Reform Act (2009) should materially restrict the FBI attempts to go beyond permissible limits of interference with basic rights. A measurable response to a serious situation. No more irregular 'fishing expeditions'. Any connection with terrorists must be proved before the arrest and charge of an individual. The Bill was to track its slow way through a medley of committees.

'Rights still an issue as FBI turns 100' was the title of a BBC Radio 4 series that first went out on 6 March 2008. A dramatic beginning was the view of Jim Weddick, a retired FBI agent of 35 years' fieldwork. Lately, as an FBI consultant, his rating of much FBI investigative work was sour – 'I think they are taking liberties and they are taking shortcuts – I was appalled'. An individual's rights must not be hazarded. Agreed, says Philip Mudd, now a senior FBI executive, quoted in the BBC programme. However, for him the new FBI, 'the world's best investigators', were, as ever, concerned about the balance between national security and civil rights. He and others spoke of the 48 years' directorship of J. Edgar Hoover, when he and his 'G men' stripped away the basic rights of real and imagined enemies of the state. Congress in 1972, dismayed at FBI excesses once arrayed against what were also then known as 'terrorists', pared away at the organisation's finances and staffing. No wonder that scant resources failed to foresee 9/11.

The charge of consistent neglect to prioritise human rights so far as possible has penetrated the core sensitivities of the FBI. Only a large-scale redevelopment programme would mend the rent fabric and reassure the public. Congress had voiced concern about what they understood as a gulf between traditional, case-bound law enforcement and intelligence-gathering operation lacking in width and too loosely related to legal criteria. The FBI, in its need for wholesale overhaul, would do well to look at the United Kingdom's MI5, perhaps not an appropriate organisational model for the United States for a myriad of reasons but they accorded a primary function to intelligence work over law enforcement. Prevention was their cardinal aim. Two other things merited attention. Were FBI field offices allowed too much latitude in counter-terrorism work? Would not a more centralised directorate in Washington integrate operations with a more dynamic, standardised approach? (Perhaps the FBI still had MI5 in mind.) Also, what was referred to as 'FBI business practice and technology' deserved a much improved coordination with federal, state and local partners.

FBI counter-terrorism is now centralised under the umbrella of the National Security Branch, set up in December 2005 in response to a presidential directive. Missions, capabilities and resources are laced together in a more modern emphasis not just on prosecution, rather on prediction and analysis. The present director of the FBI, Robert S. Mueller, assured the Senate Select Committee in January 2007 that his organisation was capable of tackling terrorism from every quarter whether it was the targeting of al-Qaida and their ideologues, or from 'homegrown radicalised' elements whose intents and capabilities were very different. In both cases, the watching and control brief of the FBI had to allow for changes in proven tactics and tradecraft, with adaptations designed to address losses in America's enhanced security measures. Jihadist groups in other places represented constant, shifting threat, where analysis and pre-emptive work need close culture-knowledgeable attention.

The CIA

Perhaps more than is the case with the FBI, the activities associated with the CIA remain essentially secretive and so prompt public speculation and some anxiety. This agency has no law enforcement function. It collects and sifts information vital to US policy formation especially in areas that effect national security and foreign affairs. Of late, the CIA has been actively reassessing its ways of working and accentuating, as required, a proactive role. No longer was this agency to be regarded as a tool of the Cold War era. Unfortunately, the White House's regard for the CIA continues to raise some doubts about its humaneness. President George Bush turned a blind eye to CIA excesses in July 2007. A new executive order of the day gave it that CIA detention and interrogation routines were fully compliant with US obligations under Article 3 of the Geneva Convention of 1949. Human Rights Watch is not at all sure about the CIA as guardian of anything. What about the incommunicado detentions, the ill-feeding of prisoners and the transfer of indictable suspects, often on flimsy grounds, to military custody at Guantanamo Bay? Is due process in these cases to be disregarded? The use of waterboarding and other torture practices, extraordinary rendition and the 'disappearing' of suspects – how does the CIA account for such things? 'By international human rights and humanitarian standards, the CIA programme is illegal to its core' is the verdict of the Human Rights Watch counter-terrorism director. Words such as these are a good deal milder than many directed at the doings and standing of the CIA.

Despite the uncertainties of the role of the CIA and a good deal of unhappiness everywhere over the agency's right-ignoring practices, President George Bush worked hard to reassert the CIA–FBI partnership in counter-terrorism strategies. Prime leadership was to be that of the CIA's Director, George Tenet, at a fine new centre in Langley, Virginia. The Terrorist Threat Integration Centre (described earlier) was to be the programme hub. An apparently rational redevelopment found some who raised doubts. Would two veteran agencies, differently modelled and led, work in absolute harmony? Might there not be cross-cutting, duplication and rivalry in the melding of two ways of working, traditional in some ways, innovative in others? Was it really wise to confer so much autonomy on one individual leader?

Of recent years, other strains have emerged – between the CIA and DOJ (Department of Justice). At times, Washington and Langley have been in vigorous dispute. At issue, usually, is the strong view of DOJ attorneys that the CIA (President's Men) is going about counter-terrorism their way and not the way of law. The DOJ is often unhappy about the CIA approach to suspect arrest and charge, its nature and timing and also about the difficulties of prescribing detention and handling it. For their part, the CIA is inclined to see judicial processes as 'a strategy of the weak'. As the President had said, it was never enough to serve our enemies with legal papers. They had declared war on the United States and war is what they got. Yet, the CIA undertaking tough counter-terrorism operations should have been more ready to recognise that it is the DOJ on 'crime watch' that helps the CIA to define and refine legitimate shaping of indictments. Ultimately, this will enable the courts to hear cases related to terrorism under three headings: (a) the Federal crime of terrorism, including material support, (b) non-terrorism criminal offences, initially with a terrorism connection, (c) an original crime charge superseded by a charge of Federal terrorism.

Put kindly, there are many in Washington who appreciate the brawn of the FBI and the CIA. 'But we do need brains and regard for rights', the DOJ adds. 'Our way is crime-hunting, "lawfare" not "warfare".'

The NSA

The 'revolutionary change' called for by the House of Representative Select Committee in July 2002 provided an impetus for, at least, evolutionary change. Aware of wide public and government dissatisfaction, the Bush Administration soon set up a Department of Homeland Security (DHS) linked to the NSA. Basically, DHS is to function as a Homeland Security Advisory System, to take on board current perceptions of terrorist threats and ways of dealing with them. Advice to the American public is relayed in three ways. First, the Homeland Security Threat Advisors broadcast 'actionable information' about incidents or targeted threats. That way, risks will be managed through readiness posture, protective action and appropriate, measured response. Second, Information Bulletins go out regularly to state authorities, private sector organisations and international partners. Contents include periodic summaries of terrorist activities, statistical reports, incident comment and warnings about known vulnerabilities. Third, there is a Colour-Coded Threat Level System communicating with safety officials and the public at large through a threat-based colour-calibrated system so that protective measures can be put in hand to reduce the likelihood or impact of an attack. The list of threat conditions relates to the significance of increasing risk. We move through Low Condition (Green) to Guarded Condition (Blue) to Elevated Condition (Yellow) to High Condition (Orange) to Severe Condition (Red).

In February 2008, the US Government's national threat level was rated as Elevated or Yellow, with a level of High or Orange for all domestic and international flights. What are Americans to do about this period of increased risk? Two things are recommended. Personal vigilance is all important: any suspicious activity must be reported. Then, everybody should put together an emergency preparedness kit. Think out an emergency plan for themselves and their family, and above all, stay informed about what to do in dire circumstances. Citizen Guidance as a Federal objective has meant that programmes for thoughtfully prepared risk management have been pushed through every home owner's letterbox. 'Preparing Makes Sense: Get Ready Now' advises you to 'stay tuned' in every practical sense.

'Staying tuned' to arrangements for personal and Federal security obligates everyone to find out what Government and police are doing to ensure protection and legality. In regard to what are termed Police Citizen Encounters, there are three tiers or categories. (The detail here could well apply also to situations in the United Kingdom.) In the first place, communication between officer and citizens is consensual, involving no coercion or liberty restraint. The second tier, a brief, minimally intrusive seizure, must be justified through reasonable suspicion of likely criminal activity. The third tier, a highly intrusive, full-scale arrest is to be based on awareness of a suspect's probable behaviour or of trustworthy information about that. Theoretically, these three tiers are there to protect rights. It is reluctantly recognised on all sides that dealing with suspected terrorism may lead on occasion to abrupt and warrantless search and seizure.

Guardianship and our rights

Quite evident in today's US press and in streetwise conversation is unease and plain protest about heightened surveillance powers granted authorities since 9/11. Is it not the case that more external restraint and intervention entangle innocent citizens and undermine precious constitutional rights to privacy and free speech? Those who are worried in this respect acknowledge that most Americans, frightened by the media bogey of Terror, seem ready to let go of privacy concerns as soon as their safety is in danger. Only a minority stands firm seeing Washington, as it were, constrained to put aside a number of checks and balances in a time of peril.

In an effort to calm public discomfiture about threatened rights, the Government put about a detailed set of reassuring statements in the summer of 2007. These were a reminder of the Administration's strategic obligations for vanquishing terrorism:

Through the freedom agenda we also have promoted the best long-term answer to al-Qaida's agenda: the freedom and dignity that comes when human liberty is protected by effective democratic institutions.

Protection in its fullest sense is the irreducible mainspring of the US Constitution. Counter-terrorism operations employing electronic surveillance and search and seizure are subject to important statutory controls. Additional restrictions limit the use of undercover enterprise to detect and prevent possible terrorist crime. Simple observation of suspects is broadly permissible but resorting to informants is subject to long-established, agency rules. There is a general requirement during surveillance and behaviour monitoring 'to minimize the intrusiveness of the operation where a private person can reasonably expect privacy'. (This is noted as 'respect for individual freedoms'.)

As one might expect, such Administration statements fail to satisfy those who consider them bland justification for measures hazarding the complete enjoyment of rights and freedoms. Human Rights Watch has consistently deplored what it considers to be the Administration's evasion or hypocrisy over statutory rights.

Afterthought

No account of counter-terrorism strategy and tactics as they are practised in two of the world's most respected democracies will allay all anxieties. Against the backcloth of threat and incident, authority has clearly cut corners and resorted to harsh, rather secretive measures with unpredictable consequences. It has not helped that President George Bush rhetorically gave emphasis to war and military might. The US Department of Justice, though, remains confident, after seven years of coping with terrorism, that flexible approaches stressing prevention and methodical disruption are more sensitive, more legal, more rational and more civilised than 'boots-and-fist-first'. Guardians of our safety are there to be held to account.

Counter-terrorism tactics and rights: the European Union

Since 2005 the EU has devised a comprehensive scheme for bringing all Member States into agreed accord to fight international terrorism. Chapter 5 looked at the legal aspects of counter-terrorism; this chapter will discuss tactical, operational measures. A common threat endangering democratic values across borders calls for decisive, coordinated action. Brussels has outlined fundamental provisions along the following lines:

■ Tightening legislation in countries where it has been weak;
■ Operational collaboration in law enforcement through Europol and Eurojust enabling arrest and prosecution of suspects;
■ Sharing intelligence and risk assessment;
■ Creating political consensus on the priority to be given to terrorist threats and on appropriate measures to deal with these;
■ Promoting the security of Europe's borders, especially of transport and communication arrangements;
■ Mutual assistance following major terrorist attacks.

A scheme such as this was put out as an 'Action Plan on Combating Terrorism' in the autumn of 2005 and in the aftermath of the Madrid bombing of 11 March 2004. Subsequently, in December 2005, it was remodelled into a new EU Counter-terrorism Strategy.

The Council of Europe had already anticipated the task of assembling a strategy in 2003 and set up a Committee of Experts on Terrorism (CODEXTER) on which all Member States would be represented. The United Kingdom's delegates are from the Home Office. Three tasks CODEXTER is working on currently are:

(1) identifying gaps in international law and action against terrorism with a view to proposing means to fill them, (2) preparing and monitoring a database of the programmes EU Members have adopted, (3) exchanging information and best practice on compensation and insurance schemes for terrorism victims.

The EU Strategy to combat terrorism internationally while respecting human freedoms, security and justice is based on four major pillars: Prevention, Protection, Pursuit and Response. These directives have much in common with those in the UK CONTEST Strategy and its '4Ps', in place since 2003. In the case of the EU primary responsibility for countering terrorism is vested in Member States but the parent Union seeks to contribute 'added value' in three main ways:

- Strengthening national capabilities, sharing knowledge and using best practice;
- Facilitating European cooperation through establishing and evaluating collaboration between security authorities and the judiciary;
- Promoting international partnership beyond the EU with the UN, other international organisations and key third countries.

Strategy and tactics are to be pursued in an accountable and democratic way. There are three institutional levels of oversight: the European Council as overlord, the European Commission and the European Parliament as regular partners in appraisal and dialogue. A security monitoring body (COREPER), continuously watches progress, implements updates and provides situation reports.

The EU, introducing the Strategy, puts emphasis on several points. Key objectives are to prevent new recruits to terrorism, to better protect potential targets, to pursue and investigate existing terrorist networking and to improve capability to respond to terrorist attack. Europe, though, is 'an area of increasing openness', which is independent and encourages unhampered movement. In these respects this is an environment where terrorists are able to exploit and abuse to further their destructive impulses. Thus, European solidarity is indispensable in dealing with a common, penetrating threat as is the building of consensus with extra-European partners. Indeed, the Strategy must be pan-national, working to resolve conflicts and to promote good governance and democracy wherever possible, in EU phrasing, 'as part of the dialogue and alliance between cultures, faiths and civilisations, in order to address the motivational and structural factors underpinning radicalisation'. Not lacking in rhetoric, the introduction brings in the four pillars of the Strategy by enumerating priorities for EU action:

Prevention

- Conditions, methods and propaganda through which terrorism draws its recruits must be identified, studied and countered in appropriate ways.

- Improvements in governance, human rights provisions, education and economic prosperity, all factors in an impoverished environment should be accounted for and, wherever possible, be aided vigorously with assistance programmes.

- A media and communication plan is urgently needed to explain to the public the necessity of EU schemes for social and economic betterment.

- Inter-cultural dialogue should address discrimination and radicalisation evident among ethnic minority groups.

Protection

- Reduction of vulnerability across Europe of critical infrastructure and specific targets. Member States have prime responsibility but collective action is vital to coordinate security across national borders;

- Methods must be developed for protecting crowded places and other 'soft' targets.

- Standards of security in air, ground and marine transport must be studied and improved.

- Prompt attention must be given to establishing adequate border controls. Closer surveillance of human and vehicle movement (with due regard for transit rights and freedoms) should lower the risk of terrorist interference.

Pursuit

- Progress in realising the four EU strategic pillars is perhaps more discernible and understandable in the case of pursuing terrorists than in the desiderata of prevention and protection. Crucially, in regard to pursuit, EU objectives are given as 'to impede terrorists' planning, to disrupt their network and the activities of recruiters to terrorism, to cut off terrorism funding and access to attack materials, and to bring them to justice while continuing to respect human rights and international law'.

- When preserving their own national security, Member States are also to focus on Union security as a whole.

- Make full use of Europol and Eurojust (described later in this chapter) to facilitate police and judicial cooperation. Continue to use the threat assessment of the European Joint Situation Centre in devising appropriate counter-terrorism measures.

- Further develop mutual recognition of judicial and administrative decisions, including the adoption of such instruments as the European Evidence Warrant and the European Arrest Warrant.

■ Financial investigation is an important part of all counter-terrorism work. The EU has already put in place scrutiny and legislation to freeze terrorist assets and to tackle illicit funding transfers and money laundering by suspect individuals and groups.

■ Deliver technical assistance to enhance the countering capabilities of key third countries.

Response

■ Response systems in place to manage the consequences of natural disasters may also be used to alleviate the effects on citizens of a terrorist attack. Revisions may be necessary to deal with unfamiliar attack methods, and their consequences. Responses should be coordinated with the action of other international organisations.

■ In the event of an incident with cross-border effects, there must be a rapid and coherent exchange of policy and operation information, media coordination and comprehensive mutual support, drawing on all available means including military resources.

■ Developing a risk-based approach to capability assessment – focusing on preparing for those events judged most likely to occur and to have great impact – will enable Member States to develop capabilities to respond in an emergency. A shared EU database listing resources and assets which Member States might be able to deploy is indispensable as is a list of possible contributions from international organisations and the UN; most useful would be the sharing of best practice and the development of suitable approaches to assistance provision to terrorism victims and their families.

To be effective and fully supported by its upholders any strategy must be continuously appraised. In the case of this comprehensive plan for action by the EU membership there is full inter-state discussion and research. After all, terrorism is well known as multi-faceted, ever changing and subject to conjecture and modification in counter methods.

The European Convention on Human Rights

Central to the counter-terrorism strategy, the employment of suitable tactics and the commitment of the EU's 27 Member States is an explicit adherence to established human rights. Founding principles in the ECHR in 1948 were laid open for state signatures in the 1950s. In all, 47 countries have ratified the Convention. These states make up the Council of Europe, a body quite separate from the EU. The Convention is divided into 'articles' setting out rights for acknowledgement and protection. From time to time this Convention has been supplemented by a number of protocols agreed by the Council of Europe, some of them guaranteeing additional rights, others to do with procedural matters.

The European Court of Human Rights, located in Strasbourg, is an international court established to interpret and apply the Convention. The Court's judges are nominated by each of the countries that are Council of Europe Members. Those who framed the EU's counter-terrorism strategy will have observed Convention articles most carefully and ensured that there was no incompatibility with Court rulings and procedures. The United Kingdom, for example, worried that some of the Strategy provisions were not altogether commensurate with ECHR principles, rectified the matter with a Human Rights Act in 2000. The UK Government justified this as an act to give greater effect to rights and freedoms guaranteed under the ECHR. In subsequent years this well-meaning assurance has been pilloried by human rights groups on a number of occasions. How is it, they ask, that UK police and security personnel get away with fragrant violation of the Act when they search premises for suspects, when they stop and search people in the streets and when they arrest and detain without a charge of terrorist intent or complicity? A positive point, though, in the case of the United Kingdom, is that courts in that country considering a possible breach of rights must take into account present and past rulings of the European Court. The Convention of 60 years ago is sill very much alive.

Council of Europe Guidelines on Rights

Several years ago, the Council of Europe instructed a ministerial committee to draw up and publish a set of guidelines on human rights and the fight against terrorism. 'Most useful those guidelines', a European Minister was heard to declare, 'now we know what to do and what not to do.' A feature of these guidelines, and a controversial one, is that while they lay down plainly and positively what must be observed, there is the understanding that in a large emergency there may have to be some degree of approved modification or 'derogation', that is, the temporary laying aside of a legal obligation.

A preamble to the Guidelines reaffirms the obligation of states to respect the ECHR and the case-law of the European Court of Human Rights in their fight against terrorism. It is interesting also to note the practical sense of committee members in stressing that measures to protect basic human rights are to exclude 'any form of arbitrariness as well as any discriminatory or racist treatment, and must be subject to appropriate supervision'. In similar vein, the Guidelines stipulated that while all counter-measures must be lawful, any necessary measure restricting human rights must define those restrictions as precisely as possible.

The Guidelines deal with measures interfering with personal privacy (body searches, house searching, bugging, surveillance of correspondence, computer material and telephone tapping) at some length. These methods must be backed up in law with explicit accounting of purpose and method and are to be challengeable in court. Arrest and police custody are also dealt with in the Guidelines. Only reasonable suspicion is to justify summary arrest in regard to terrorist activity. Those arrested must be told the reason for the action. Any custody must be of short duration with a prompt court appearance before a judge. Once again, a detainee may challenge lawfulness.

A person accused of terrorist involvement benefits from the presumption of innocence. Anyone so accused has the right to a fair hearing before an independent, impartial law tribunal and no time is to be lost in guaranteeing their basic right. A suspect is to be protected against unfairness, however vague or heinous the testimony against him/her and however difficult it may be to obtain reliable evidence for the defence. Extradition requests, for example, are always to be refused where the would-be receiving state has a questionable human rights record.

The issues to do with derogation are causing concern across Europe. Derogation is the permitting of a state to stand aside from its major obligations (to quote the Council of Europe):

when the fight against terrorism takes place in a situation of war or public emergency which threatens the life of a nation, a State may adopt measures temporarily derogating from certain obligations ensuing from the international instruments of protection of human rights, to the extent of the exigencies of the situation, as well as within the limits under the conditions fixed by international law. The State must notify the authorities of the adoption of such measures in accordance with the relevant international instruments.

Never, however is a state to derogate from the right to life, from the prohibition against torture, inhuman, degrading treatment or punishment of suspects. Regular reassessment of circumstances is necessary, the Council states, so that when they improve, derogation can be lifted.

The straight thinking behind this stipulation is plain enough. Why, then, does the UK Government continue to practise detention without appeal or trial, something inimical to Article 5 of the European Human Rights Convention and its right to liberty? Were there so few legislators with calm minds in the autumn of 2001 and 9/11? London has said that indefinite detention requires a long-term derogation from the country's human rights obligations. The threat justifying their legal withdrawal is still there.

The arguments as to the possible turning down of extradition demands and the carefulness over derogation seems reasonable, though the Guidelines' terms 'exigencies' and 'imperatives' are debatable. Should a suspect ever be deprived of freedom on somebody else's say-so? How far do EU 'guarantees' go? It is seldom possible for a suspect to initiate a (legal) challenge to those arresting him, detaining him or preferring a charge.

Counter-terrorism tactics: permissible ones

It is now more than five years since the Council of Europe's Committee of Ministers had in mind the task of identifying counter-terrorism tactics which might not be admissible, given the all-importance of safeguarding basic human rights. A Multi-disciplinary Group on International Action against Terrorism was put together and, after preliminary investigations, their job was moved over to CODEXTER. The experts were to look closely at the special investigation techniques commonly in use. Should not standards and safeguards be defined to ensure that usage complied with ECHR requirements?

Foremost in the enquiry was a definition and listing of special investigation techniques. Looked at in the main were electronic surveillance, interception of communications, searches of persons, vehicles and premises, agents provocateurs and planted informants. This was not an easy task, given the complexity of tactics and instruments. The measures under consideration are either overtly or secretly used. The Committee could hardly disguise the fact that special investigative measures, designed to provide incriminating material, will often violate fundamental rights and freedoms, such as respect for private life, and also impinge upon certain principles of criminal-law procedures, such as fairness in the gathering of evidence. The element of secrecy normally associated with these procedures does not much appeal to lawyers or to judges. Frequently, such evidence is not easy to corroborate. Apart from this, the 27 legal systems of EU Member States almost certainly have different means of dealing with evidence. The ministerial Committee, treading carefully here, was unanimous in requiring secret-style evidence gathering to have legal backing. The Committee was acquainted with the case-law finding of the European Court of Human Rights that there is no absolute prohibition of reliance on inference. Terrorist intent or behaviour is on many occasions inferred. The question is plain: what really are the guiding principles of investigative tactics?

No guidelines will ever dismiss speculation among politicians, lawyers and laymen. Ideally, counter-terrorism programmes will be proactive. The activating chief principle has to do with 'exceptional circumstances' where there is a 'reasonable suspicion' that an offence may be committed. Inference again. The EU regards this mega-principle as divisible into three sub-principles:

- The sub-principle of subsidiarity where particular tactics may be used only if no other, less intrusive methods enable the offence to be prevented or detected;
- The sub-principle of proportionality where particular tactics may be used only if safeguarding of public order overrides the protection of private life in general;
- The sub-principle of specificity where information gathered in the use of particular tactics may be used only in support of the charge which led to their being used.

Radicalisation and recruitment

In November 2007, the EU published proposals to address radicalisation and recruitment to terrorism. An urgent priority is somehow to prevent young men from being taken up into networks of violent extremism. Much was made earlier, in 2005, of enacting strong penalties against 'incitement'. What, though, is meant by 'incitement'? How far does legitimate criticism go? What are the tolerable bounds of protests and demonstrations? Europe's police and interior ministries have wrestled with contentious definitions. Public announcement of action plans has been sporadic and enterprising journalists have had to quarry wide for detail. Incitement and its bedfellow, radicalisation, will be subject to media surveillance, above all, of the Internet, and legal action taken against extremist propaganda. There will be much close contact with ethnic political groups and religious affiliations, to attempt to stem terrorist recruitment. One or two possibly repressive steps will be put in hand. Data-retention will monitor emails and telephone calls where there is suspect communication.

Trans-European watchfulness will be able to use the European Arrest Warrant to replace traditional extradition procedures in the case of a suspect's arrest and the European Evidence Warrant for presentation in court. Apart from Watch the Web there will be a Watch the Money to block money transfers regarded as funding for terrorist activities.

Throughout the Guidelines discussed above, there is the red thread of the state's obligation to protect itself against proscribed groups over against the other obligation of honouring basic human rights. The juxtaposition of these obligations is difficult and, at times, controversial. A point about this juxtaposition, and one not easing it, is that in August 1990 the European Court of Human Rights ruled that terrorist crime fell into a special category which forced the police to act quickly to exploit information in order to lessen the risk of suffering and loss of life. Additional resources would go to Europol (the European Police Office, a system to coordinate the work of European Police and the EU criminal law enforcement agency).

Earlier in this chapter, reference was made to the European Arrest Warrant and to the institution of Eurojust. These two are important innovations. The Warrant was introduced by the European Council in June 2002; it enables wanted persons to be transferred directly from one judicial authority to another, with due regard for the arrested person's fundamental rights. Remarkable, too, the Warrant goes further in changing the nature of legal cooperation in Europe from conventional collaboration to unqualified, mutual recognition and acceptance of court decisions in other Member States. Then there is Eurojust, a pan-European body acting as coordinator in the legal field, facilitating interaction between the judicial authorities of different EU Member States' legal systems. Where Europol police collaboration essentially puts into effect security tactics on the ground, Eurojust's lawyers at their desks make sure that legal instruments are framed in accord and practised in unison.

EU Commissioner for Justice, Freedom and Security, Franco Frattini, and colleagues have been eager to describe the sharing of counter-terrorism know-how and experience with the United States. The EU signed six groundbreaking agreements with Washington within three years of 9/11. Ministerial liaison across the Atlantic is expressed by regular, policy dialogue, working parties in session and posting of staff to offices in the two continents. European and American law enforcement authorities sieve, assess and act upon 'sensitive' information (once stringent, EU personal data standards were insisted upon). An extradition accord brings up to date and harmonises existing extradition agreements. Integrated policies to do with air traffic and ground transport and their inspection and security control across borders have been seen too. On the other hand, it has not been easy to align the distinctive working of FBI and CIA headquarters with counterparts in European intelligence services. There were impediments to European court use of some types of information like phone taps and implanted informers. Information sharing, in view of its diverse and sometimes questionable origin, took a long time to achieve accord. There was always in the background discontinued unease that Washington too often views terrorism as something to be approached though military means rather than by, admittedly, slower political action and law enforcement. The US rendition programme of transferring terrorist suspects to other countries with less than adequate human rights records has encountered a great deal of EU criticism. The Bush Administration, in strongly supporting intercontinental cooperation, must have hoped that this would help authorities on both sides keep better track of suspected terrorist and also prevent them from entering the United States.

EU counter-terrorism: some state programmes

The larger EU Members have carefully designed counter-terrorism programmes. The publication of the EU Strategy in 2005 was followed, a year later, by a meeting in Paris of foreign ministers and ministers responsible for security. They were to undertake a thorough review of new trends in terrorism throughout the world. Their discussions underscored agreement to find solutions, taking account of all the factors likely to ensure a lasting settlement of unresolved conflicts and the need for seeing to circumstances which could nurture the development of terrorism. Action plans setting out a list of 25 agreed counter-terrorism measures were then made available to the public. This initiative brought 27 nations together, as they say, 'in order to harness our own capacities more tightly [it was] decided to establish among our countries a directory of counter-terrorism competencies, skill and expertise to facilitate practical cooperation'. Since numerous countermeasures have to be brought on board in secret, the actions lack incisive detail, perhaps inevitably. A number of what the EU terms 'state profiles' indicate directions to be taken.

France

Legal attention to acts of terrorism has recently been modified and is central to a law of 9 March 2004. Great stress is laid on investigators having clear authorisation from magistrates (an authoritative caucus in France) before they can conduct surveillance. Absolute regard for suspects' human rights is always emphasised explicitly, as are the necessities of justifying a security operation and of setting that within a time limit. Problems arose when the Government wanted to introduce a longer duration in police custody for terrorist suspects. Two extra 24-hour extensions would be possible where a terrorism threat was suspected and, in addition, in a crisis situation police could have a further 24 hours. These extensions would bring to six days the total time a suspect could be held before a hearing with a magistrate. Nor would there be any guarantee of access to counsel and to judicial supervision. Human Rights Watch led sustained opposition to these proposals seeing them as quite incompatible with French obligations under international human rights law. Robust procedures must safeguard presumption of innocence, the right to adequate defence and trial and that of being able to challenge detention. The sub-principles of subsidiarity and of proportionality are vital requirements before preventive measures are applied. The law of 2004 reminds security authorities that the judiciary is 'the guardian of individual liberty' in the words of Article 66 of the French Constitution.

France is very much in favour of collaboration with other states and a useful Franco-Spanish investigation-and-control system is now in operation. Nearer home, Paris has not found it easy to overcome hierarchies and departmental rivalries in bringing its ministries into joint working.

Germany

Prosecution of terrorist criminal offences is a matter exclusively for the Federal Public Prosecutor General. It was found necessary to review and amend domestic anti-terrorist legislation to ensure that terrorist acts are established as 'serious criminal offences' and that the seriousness of such acts is duly reflected in the sentence served. An extra legal provision was to make sure that Federal law enabled Berlin to investigate and, if necessary, indict organisations or associations which appear to be used as cover for terrorist activity. An innovation in recent years has been the methodical cultivation of police liaison with other European capitals. There is a very clear emphasis on collaboration with Europol and association with Eurojust. German law and practice do not make so much of human rights preservation as do the French. It is clear, however, that the very strict regulations covering authorisation of investigative tactics and their permissible limits do mean that citizens' fundamental rights are being upheld. Liberal criticism of the Government's comprehensive security arrangements in the Security Package of 2005 focused on what were thought to be repressive measures against asylum seekers and foreign workers and, too, the possibility of fuelling Islamophobia. Government reassurances seem to have mollified critics. Apart from this there is a certain amount of anxiety in some quarters that German links with the CIA rendition programme are too close and that illegal transport of terrorism suspects has used German airports.

Italy

Security operations and the work of law enforcement, in general, must be accountable in considerable detail to legal officers. Any evasion in notification is punishable. The law of 2001, particularly referring to terrorist 'crime' and its code for Penal Procedures, has been meticulously framed. Authorisation for preventive and protective measures will be granted security personnel if they respect human rights and individual freedoms – the principle sanctioned by Italy's constitution. A point Italians make easily is that after years of dictatorship the citizen has to be watchful about any authoritarian tendencies in government, leading to erosion of civil and fundamental rights, so, naturally, the current stringent counter-terrorist measures worry many people. It is a fact, of concern to the Berlusconi Administration, that Italy has an abundance of extreme political parties. Controversy has grown strongly where legitimate rights of admission and residence for non-Italians are being set in balance by the security service, suspecting that those hospitable rights are being taken advantage of for terrorist purposes. Policing is frequently accused of being discriminatory, with brusque stop-and-search, street arrests and swift deportations.

Netherlands

Dutch Codes of Criminal Procedure are clear, consistent and frequently updated. Rather like French practice, subsidiarity and proportionality sub-principles are essential pre-conditions for approved countering operations. These principles may be seen as tactical considerations rather than ethical ones. Dutch counter-terrorism is in the hands of a very strong and resourceful General Intelligence and Security Service (AIVD), which describes its approach as 'wide range', employing a range of instruments and organisations in concert – political, administrative, financial, religious and legal – all bearing down collaboratively on those social and cultural problems that incline towards separatism and possible violence. There is a mission in the Government to foresee possible radicalisation and recruitment of extreme elements, especially in the Netherlands' crowded and polyglot urban communities. Rather like Italy, the Netherlands is traditionally a transit zone with easy access and a multi-ethnic population. A major effort, therefore, goes in to aspects of transportation security via road, rail and air. Control through inspection and monitoring is very efficient. Quite recently the Netherlands has introduced a nationwide Counter-terrorism Alert System to alert business companies and local authorities to impending terrorist threats and to enable participants to take necessary security measures expeditiously and to increase resilience. There are four states of alert: standard, low, moderate and high. In contrast to many countries, this is not a public alert system, rather it is designed to warn and protect critical components in the economic and local government infrastructure.

Spain

Specific counter-terrorism operations are a prime feature of legislation dated 21 May 2003. Criminal procedures arrowed at terrorists approved a range of investigative routines provided that their tactical use is not injurious to a Spaniard's basic human rights. There are perhaps controversial references to 'exigencies' and 'special security circumstances', which may not calm the anxieties of some critics in Madrid. Many in Spain have not found it easy to forget or recover from the terrorist bombings in the capital in 2004 and they may well feel that the threats of terrorism justify 'hard', perhaps repressive, counter action. Even so, the Spanish Government has emphasised its concern to uphold basic freedoms as far as possible and also to treat suspects fairly. It has not been easy to deal with Spain's considerable Islamic population, given that fundamentalist ideologies are transported so directly across the Mediterranean. It has surprised nobody that the Spanish Government lost no time in 2004, the year of the Madrid train outrage, in peremptorily initiating a system of swift deportation to get rid of those foreign nationals considered 'troublemakers'. Expulsion would be a better word. A particular issue in debate is whether the Spanish Government, in ordering deportation, is quite certain that nobody will be returned to a place where they may be tortured.

Sweden

Traditionally, respect for human rights and freedoms is strongly marked in Scandinavia. Stockholm's position is that restorative interference and intrusion are only permissible if reasons for this are made absolutely clear. Only extraordinary threats to daily life and the infrastructure can justify vigorous counter action at the expense of privacy and freedom of movement, speech and association. The Parliamentary ombudsman an official who acts as interpreter of regulations and as go-between in individual–authority problems and disputes, as well as the Chancellor of Justice exercise keen scrutiny and possible intervention where any security control is mooted and practised. They are careful to examine all requests for security clearance and are solidly backed up by counter-terrorism legislation from 2002 and 2004.

Retrospect: Europe right or wrong?

Fine, many will say, fine that Europe has in place a Strategy to fight the terrorist. It seems a workable compilation with reasonably clear objectives and a line-out of priorities to attain targets. Prevention, Protection and Pursuit are there in a full programme to further our security and at least 27 nations have made up a partnership in support. It is fine, too, that the EU is determined to uphold our basic human rights and freedoms. Then there are the Guidelines to underwrite the need to ensure the fundamental rights laid down in the European Human Rights Convention of 1948.

At first glance, indeed, things appear very much in order. Longer, careful study and consideration of what is happening in today's world bring second thoughts. Statements in the Strategy and Guidelines refer to the 'impetus' of counter-terrorism operations as perhaps leading to rights restriction, perhaps only temporary, and even to derogation. The statements are phrased guardedly but this may not dispel anxiety as to their implementation. Thus, how many terrorist suspects are presumed innocent at whatever stage of enquiry and detention? As for the processes governing extradition requests, are those liable for transfer likely to see themselves as pawns in inter-state negotiation? What, moreover, is the state security that Member States are supposed to ensure? Could that ever be at the expense of some personal, individual security?

There appears to be a fair amount of controversy in regard to counter-terrorism and ethnic minorities. One European commentator, Mats Engström, a member of the editorial staff of *Aftonbladet*, a leading Swedish newspaper, has squared up to some of the issues raised. How can the fight against terrorism and its wellspring – militant fundamentalism – succeed, he asks, when so many Muslims in Europe feel that authorities in general, and the police in particular, see them as security risks? When discrimination is part of everyday life? If only all kinds of terrorism were treated equally, European governments would then be doing more to stop the daily insults to many Muslims. Engström and others certainly often see European government policies as counterproductive. By focusing on Islamic extremism, the suspicion among Muslims that they are being treated differently could be strengthened, in fact, confirming the world view that extremists are keen to communicate. Demonising Muslims in general or too much talk about cultural tension encourages populist politicians in a dangerous game. Many young men will feel themselves treated as second-class citizens, especially if they encounter intrusive surveillance.

Governments in the United Kingdom, France and Germany are not unaware of apparent ethnic discrimination and the birth of radicalism. In late February 2008, UK senior police officers drew up a plan seeking to prevent Muslims from turning to violence. Each part of the United Kingdom was mapped for its potential to produce extremists and supporters for al-Qaida. The police believe that new recruits to possible terrorism are being attracted to it, despite scores of convictions, arrests and the disruption of terrorist plots. There is a pressing need, so it is urged, to develop the growing relationships between the police and local communities at every level with regard to preventing the indoctrination of violent extremism.

On the whole, the EU approach to dangerous radicalisation looks good on paper but in fact the inter-cultural dialogue it espouses has hardly been attempted. An ambitious programme launched in November 2007 provides for taking possible action against extremism in media sources such as Internet monitoring, online surveillance of personal computers and a degree of case-specific watching of emails and telephone calls. Understandably, these countering proposals have met sharp criticism from those who sense in such measures as these the real possibilities of authority attempting to stifle legitimate freedom of expression. The EU, in principle and practice, is trying hard to dissuade likely terrorists and to reassure the public in various ways. On balance, strategy and tactics are making some ground, inch by inch, amid a welter of suggestion and debate.

8

Counter-terrorism: treatment of suspects

'They're treating me as a terrorist suspect. What rights to I have? How do I stand in regard to likely charges, detention, and possible imprisonment?' These questions form the stuff of this chapter and they are considered chiefly in the context of UK and US procedures.

Arrest

A senior police officer recently spoke of arrest as settling nothing and questioning everything. 'What could they have done to prevent it?' is a most often heard question. Arrest statistics are interesting. Under the sweeping Terrorism Act 2000, there were in the year 2005–6 some 44,503 stop-and-search events in the United Kingdom. Of these, 105 led to an arrest. That is only 1 in every 400 people stopped. Was this perhaps a disproportionate outcome because the officer pulling somebody up was too hasty and over-zealous in his 'reasonable suspicion' and discretion? Or was it because criminal intent was lacking? In the City of London in the same period there were 6,846 stoppings. In this case, no evidence was found to justify any arrest.

A further look at the 2005–6 figures may yield something for reflection. The 44,503 figure was an advance of 34 per cent over the previous year. Inside this total, Asians faced an increase of

84 per cent, black people an increase of 51 per cent, search of 'other' ethnic groups rose 36 per cent and white people met an increase of 24 per cent. More than half of all stop-and-search was in London. Again, why the lack of proportion? This is an issue worth some thought. Moreover, there is virtually nothing to show that any of the 105 arrested were later convicted on a terrorist charge. Several high-ranking officers in London's Metropolitan Police Service have said that random stop-and-search operations do more harm than good. If black people are seven times more likely to be stopped than white people, is this not likely to arouse protest about unfair discrimination and to lessen trust in the arm of the law?

Muslims are acutely aware of their liability to be stopped, and even arrested. Positively, the Muslim Council of Britain, which claims to represent 400 affiliated smaller groups, robustly appealed in July 2007 to all Muslims to cooperate readily with police. It was unacceptable, they said, that any faith should bear responsibility for the action of a few extremists they had never met. Any of the majority was just as likely to be victim of barbarous terrorism as anybody else. Although there are Muslim members of the reported 200 organisations suspected of extremist orientation which have been proscribed by Whitehall, almost all Muslims reject jihadist talk. They deplore the ranting of certain imams in one or two of the United Kingdom's 1,600 mosques and think of this as inflammatory.

Ways and means of lessening the number of Muslims arrested are to be found in a plan announced in August 2007 by Scotland Yard. Tarique Ghaffur, Assistant Commissioner and Britain's most senior Asian police officer, designed a scheme for a 'safety foundation' to identify extremists who are likely even to look 'arrestable'. Young men, chiefly, will be 'debriefed' as fully and as sensitively as possible with the stress on 'working out' their dissatisfaction, even anger, and reducing the alienation that may push them towards violence. The scheme is to be focused on the mixed communities where ethnic discrimination, even racial tension, is found to be a problem. Muslim case-workers are to shoulder responsibility for initiation, development and progress reports. A police point of view about this scheme of proactive engagement is that it is better to work early with a community than have to go a long way later with blue lamps flashing. Perhaps seen as a method experiment in a hearts-and-minds approach, it is a step towards those Home Office strategy pillars of Prevention and Protection. One of Ghaffur's Muslim colleagues reminds us that his people frequently refer to their UK home as '*daral-sulh*' roughly, 'the land of contract', where Muslims contractually value and obey the law in exchange for a guarantee of liberty and protection.

The notions outlined so far have to do with generality. For the individual recognised as a suspect, the question of rights is crucial. Successive governments in London have enacted, modified and re-enacted stipulations aimed at clarifying a suspect's rights.

The Police and Criminal Evidence Act 1984 and its associated Codes of Practice aimed to strike a balance between community interests and the liberties and other rights of those taken in as suspect individuals. Subsequent amendments and the Criminal Justice Act 2003 put plenty of significance into the position of the individual-at-risk.

Charges

'What exactly is a terrorist?' The key word in a question often asked is 'exactly'. As one would expect, the called-for precision in that word defeats most people. An attempted answer invariably has much of the answerer's attitudes and personality in it. For the lawyer to move into the realm of preferring a charge or, at any rate, assisting in that process, there are distinctive ethical and political reservations to bear in mind. In the field of counter-terrorism, what is proposed and augmented in practice ought to be tightly undergirded by legislation. Most states, in an approach to making a terrorist charge of an individual or named group, then come up against the criterion of 'exactness' and the clear fact that there is very little consistent precision to confirm what the law requires. Rosalind Higgins, an eminent international lawyer, wondered, in 1997, whether what is termed counter-terrorist 'law' is not the expression of community condemnation. If so, that is not easily fitted into what lawyers need and expect for decisive implementation. Possibly they have to fall back more on ethical considerations?

The alleged terrorist facing a charge based on this vague term 'terrorism' could at least be thought to be lacking the social power and skills needed to effect social or political change peacefully. Militant, perhaps violent, action is the sole recourse. What, though, is militancy? It is violence that is the crime. In most legal systems protest action if non-violent is not legally actionable. Moral justifications to reinforce a charge or deny it will be common. Albert Bandura (1998) pointed out that the 'moral encrustation' around a charge of violent protest poses more troublesome problems for democratic societies than for totalitarian ones. He sees terrorists as wielding greater power over a nation that places high value on human life and is thereby constrained in the way it responds. There will generally be political content to the less-than-exactness of the judicial process. Histrionic and emotional elements are likely to invade the straight, sanitised work of the courtroom. A leader in a November 2006 edition of *The Guardian* instanced the case of Dhiren Barot, up for the charge of terrorism. In imposing a life sentence for murder conspiracy, was Mr Justice Butterfield wise in referring to Barot and his associates as 'seeking to bring death and destruction to the Western world'? Outside the courtroom, Barot's confederates could see the prisoner as a man with a mission. No common criminal this, rather, a hero and a martyr. Misplaced reference? Does the charge of terrorism reverberate in other than legal ways? The point is arguable.

Nature of charges

Just a sample of terrorist charges brought in recent years illustrates differences in meaning. Conspiracy to murder heads the list. There follow conspiracy to cause explosions likely to endanger life, incitement to commit an act of terrorism, the possession of terrorism-related materials (aspiring bomb makers), soliciting murder, inciting racial hatred, incitement to murder, conspiracy to commit a public nuisance and murder and offences under the Explosive Substances Act 1883 (the list is in some order of frequency). A number of other offences for which individuals have been charged show not only diversity but must lead one to wonder how guilt was ever proven. In the years 2000 what can 'incitement to treason' mean? What of the violence that was or was not contrived in such offences as 'criminal damage' and 'aggravated trespass' and, perhaps more debatably, in 'possession of offensive weapons'? A charge that the prosecution invariably made was that those hauled before a court were 'preparing an act of terrorism'.

The charge of 'preparing' actually went badly wrong on one occasion in January 2008. A 19-year-old girl student cycling near Heathrow was stopped, arrested and charged under Section 58 of the Terrorism Act 2000. She was held in a local police cell for 30 hours. The charge was that of collecting information likely to be of use to persons committing or preparing an act of terrorism. Eventually, her local newspaper was helpful in ridiculing the affair and led her to appeal successfully on the grounds of harassment, obstruction and gross interference with privacy. Stout defence of human rights won the day – as it should.

Court procedure

The charge, of course, must be taken up into court procedure. In the drama-filled days of 2005 and the urgency of pressing charges against those considered responsible for incidents, there was some controversy not only about precise definition but also about the type of court that charging should employ. In some quarters there was outrage, if not apoplexy, at the reported Home Office idea that special courts might be established. Sitting in secret, courts were to determine how long suspects could be detained without specific charge. They would be given in-camera access to sensitive intelligence and phone-tap evidence which, at any rate in 2005, could not be presented in court. Another notion from the Home Office was the use of security-vetted 'special advisors' as legal representatives of those detained. Just as innovative, and quite unacceptable to lawyers, was a suggestion from Tony Blair, Prime Minister, and himself a barrister, that revised court procedures allow a pre-trial process. This would provide a way for police and security service requests for detention before charge to be extended from the then current 14 days to 90 days. In the event, neither lawyers nor Members of Parliament could stomach this and the suggestion was consigned to the bin, amid government embarrassment over a heavy Commons defeat.

Skirting the conventions of English court procedure was bound to lead to anguish in legal chambers and in press rooms. Again, in 2005, there was pressure to charge members of certain organisations deemed to be broadcasting a politically radical message. It was never quite clear what sort of charge could be directed at someone rated as a dissident. How was it they were dissident? Could they be accused of 'radical extremism'? Suppose it were non-violent? The Terrorism Act 2000 only allowed 'terrorist organisations' to be banned. A proposal to ban an Islamic group like Hisb-ut-Tahir and to charge its adherents required further primary legislation. Would the British National Party, extreme as they were, be considered a terrorist group?

The idea of secret court procedures never gained momentum. A dramatic departure from the United Kingdom's 'adversarial' justice system, with defence and prosecution sparring in the open, would give way to something approaching, say, the French inquisitorial model, where the examining magistrate hears evidence from witnesses and suspects, orders searches and authorises warrants before deciding whether there is a valid case for promoting a watertight charge. Of course, this approach could dismiss the risk of leakage of sensitive information. Yet, can a suspect refute allegations if he/she is in ignorance of the charge?

Not only do lawyers find inexactness over terrorism charges unhelpful. Juries, too, are sometimes perplexed. An instance of this is the case of the four men who set out on 21 July 2005 to bomb London's transport. This would have been a repetition of the heinous bombing of 7 July which had caused many casualties. The four were arrested as terrified passengers fled the compartment of an Underground train. The charges brought were those of conspiracy to murder and conspiracy to cause an explosion. The trial was to last six months. Two of the accused claimed that their bombing was a protest against the war in Iraq. They had never intended their demonstration to lead to death and injury. Despite the evidence, the jury was able to agree on a unanimous verdict in the case of two of the accused four. These two were remanded, pending a fresh trial before the end of 2007. The judge was in no doubt about the guilt of the four. They had, he said, been 'controlled and directed by al-Qaida'. The defendants had known exactly the result of their abominable action. Given life sentences, they would not be considered for parole for at least 40 years.

Something similar had happened in Spain in January 2007, after the bombing of trains in a Madrid railway station. The jury, who had been sitting for four months, were unsure about the terrorism guilt of 7 out of 28 before them. The judge, on the other hand, was convinced of their guilt so surely that he sentenced 2 of the bombers to an impressive term of 34,000 years. They were to serve at least 40 years before any release.

Alienation

Counter-terrorism measures and the charges that are levelled inevitably lead to discomfort, anxiety and disruption of normal life. Nowhere are feelings about this more clear than among those groups newly arrived in the United Kingdom and among those who have already put down their roots. Muslims, in particular, sense discrimination in official policy. Most unease, often erupting in anger, is seen among those from Jordan, Libya, Algeria, Lebanon and Syria, whose home regions are often seen as terrorist recruiting grounds. Former nationals of these countries accuse the United Kingdom of double standards: of 'cosying up' overseas to those doubtful regimes in the hope of getting lucrative trade contracts while the new British residents are treated as 'most suspicious'. Pakistanis, especially in London, feel quite desperate about their troublemaker image in the eyes of the capital. They are inclined, though, to accept the general verdict that a reputation for instinctive violence may have an origin in the alienation of Pakistani youth in the United Kingdom and the failure of their families to assimilate. 'Why don't you treat us as equals?' is a poignant rejoinder.

Liberal concerns regard the UK Government as too complacent about community alienation. Looking at contemporary London, Amnesty International sees 'a dangerous imbalance between draconian actions taken in the name of security and an obligation to protect human rights'. These means tarnish the UK's image and its ability to promote fundamental freedoms. Lord Paddy Ashdown remarks on a failure to build trans-ethnic understanding. 'We concentrate almost all our efforts on the short-term struggle to prevent the next outrage and almost none on the long-term task of winning the hearts and minds of moderate Islamists'. Realistically, the United Kingdom's 2 million Muslims, far from being the country's problem, are an essential part of the best defence against future attacks. Since 2006, a project entitled 'Islamophobia – Don't Suffer in Silence' has been underway in three London boroughs, West Yorkshire and Lancashire. The main aim is to encourage Muslims to be more able and willing to report incidents and crimes they believe are directed against them. It is also hoped to bring about clear links between police and local Muslims and, further, to raise awareness of Islamophobia among security service personnel. The reporting initiative is regarded as a valuable complement to existing work done by community and ethnic associations.

A government ploy in early 2008 was to suggest to officials dealing with security matters that they could talk to Muslims about the nature of terrorist threats without implying that Muslims are in some way to blame. Terms such as 'Islamist extremism' or 'jihad-fundamentalist' must be avoided. Talk of a struggle for values or a battle of ideas sounds less confrontational, if the idea of shared values is used and explored. Certainly, where terrorist charges have been directed at Muslims, it is vital to set the nature and extent of them in proportion so that fellow-Muslims do not see themselves as excluded. Home Office advice is that an approach such as this must be a deliberate attempt to 'engage' any who feel victimised. People stop listening if they think they are being attacked. Careful listening to others can be an imperative weapon in a counter-terrorism arsenal.

Detention

The 'Battle of the Tearooms' was now in full swing. In early 2008 this was the name given by Members of Parliament to the frequent visits to the House by Shami Chakrabarti, Director of the Human Rights group Liberty and a former Home Office barrister. Members were buttonholed politely and then asked how they felt about the Government's intention later in 2008 to push for an extension to the established detention period. What would their position be in the face of the proposal to raise the current detention limit from 28 days to 41 days? The Terrorism Act 2006 had brought in the 28-day term replacing the 7 days permitted under the Criminal Justice Act 2003. If the proposal were not carried then the Prime Minister, Gordon Brown, would encounter his first parliamentary defeat since taking over at Downing Street. It was reckoned in March 2008 that one in three Members might fail to support extension. They could not easily countenance the idea of detaining terrorist suspects for such a long period. Party loyalists were grappling with their conscience.

The Government declared it needed new extension powers for exceptional circumstances when police must unravel complicated plots and that would not be easy within the present 28-day period. Many people were not convinced that Whitehall had any credible case for extension. Scotland Yard, naturally, was in favour but not the Director of Public Prosecutions, Sir Ken Macdonald, nor the former Lord Chancellor, Lord Falconer, nor the former Attorney General, Lord Goldsmith. Lord Chief Justice, Lord Woolf opposed the bid. Former MI5 executives, Lady Manningham-Buller and Stella Rimmington found further extension unprincipled and impractical. Across the House even the Shadow Home Secretary, David Davis, believing the Government had failed to persuade its own side, resigned to fight an unopposed by-election. The odds were that the Government would be defeated over 'a massive erosion of people's liberties and rights under the law'. Feeling cornered, Whitehall insisted that this was no 'massive erosion'. Only a small number of terrorist suspects, generally less than 50, would be held for a maximum spell with perhaps only a dozen or so being charged with the rest released. Moreover, the current detention regime had not been challenged in the courts. Statements of this ilk were seen by opponents as dodging principles and as offensive to basic freedoms. Why did no other country resort to such questionable practice and to such lame justifications?

Shami Chakrabarti and others, in and out of government, supposed that a compromise might be possible, a calm consensus putting forward alternative policies more within fair-trial conditions rather than have injustice and the losing of hearts and minds. Backbenchers began to show interest in a tabled amend-ment refuting a 'take it or leave it' proposal and emphasising modifications which would give Parliament a far greater role in the oversight of detention policy. Only if 41 days were absolutely necessary as a temporary emergency stratagem would House of Commons endorsement be secured and that would depend upon careful examination and debate.

Compromise or no there was a fairly solid phalanx of opposition within Parliament and in the country. The Home Secretary, Jacqui Smith found it quite difficult to firm up arguments for any extension of pre-charge detention. Liberty pressed her hard in interview and in correspondence. Rather than the Government's blanket extension all that was needed was for the Department of Public Prosecutions and a police chief to report that extension of a particular suspect's detention would materially advance their investigation. What alternatives were there? Liberty suggested more post-charge questioning once a person had been officially and properly charged with a terrorist offence. There must be judi-cial safeguards. In the event, the Government Bill to detain for 42 days before being charged was passed by a tiny majority, thanks, many allege, to House of Commons back-room dealing. It was in October 2008 that the House of Lords threw out the Bill quite conclusively, by two to one, and the 28-day period remains.

Tearoom meetings and banner-waving demonstrations are a feature of contemporary disquiet over detention extension. Few have forgotten the drama of December 2004 when, a week before Christmas, the House of Lords ruled eight to one in favour of appeals by nine terrorist detainees. Eight Law Lords were insistent that certain UK anti-terrorism measures, for instance, lengthy detention without charge, were incompatible with European human rights laws. When the nine were first detained in the summer of 2002 they had taken their cases to the Special Immigration Appeals Commission. This Commission ruled that anti-terrorism detention discriminated against any who were foreign nationals. This ruling was later overturned by the Court of Appeal who found that there was now a state of emergency threatening the nation's life. Not deterred by that, the nine returned in 2004 to the House of Lords, the United Kingdom's highest court. A senior Law Lord there, Lord Nicholls of Birkenhead, spoke of the men's case in these words:

'Indefinite imprisonment without charge or trial is anathema in any country which observes the rule of the law. It deprives the detained person of the protection a criminal trial is intended to afford'. Terrorists or not, the Lords were firm in their judgements. The Government must pay the appeals costs.

All too clearly, extending detention arouses public opposition, even anger. Before the Lords' judgement Amnesty International wrote to them arguing that the detentions were not at all in the spirit of ATCSA. The very indefiniteness of detention was surely criminal in violating the right of fair trial. The secrecy resorted to in all government procedures was reprehensible in keeping suspects and their legal counsel quite in the dark. Defenders and critics of extension were digging in their positions resolutely. Several peers in the House of Lords, though not judges, were heard to remark that the real threat to the life of the nation, its laws and political values was as much from our own repressive legislation as from any terrorist.

A final point about terrorist detention in the United Kingdom is a statement from the Ministry of Justice in March 2005. There is an 'urgent requirement' to give priority to the control of extremist prisoners and to counter their likely hyper-radical influence over other prisoners. The number of those convicted for terrorist-related crimes or on remand has already reached 130 and is expected to grow as a number of high-profile trials are concluded. Security services have already fastened upon more than 2,000 individuals they regard as potential terrorists.

Detention spells in other states

What is the position in other countries exercising the pre-charge detention? It is helpful to read the Liberty report of November 2007, *Terrorism Pre-charge Detention: Comparative Law Study*, a far-ranging authoritative survey of detention in 15 countries. The number of permitted days varies very considerably: in the United Kingdom it is 28 days, in the United States 2 days, in Canada 1 day, in Australia 12 days and in South Africa 2 days. France limits the stint to 6 days, Turkey to $7^{1}/_{2}$ days and Spain to 4 days. In respect of figures such as these Liberty's question is stern: 'How can our government and some police argue that the United Kingdom needs to hold people for a month when so many other countries manage pre-charge detention periods of less than one week?' All countries face the threat of terrorism inspired by al-Qaida. Many have suffered attacks recently and the loss of hundreds of lives. Police everywhere face the same investigative problems that are cited in Britain to support much longer detention. Given the disparity of detention provision and the UK's staunch reliance on 28 days there is, in Liberty's view, an understandable inclination for radical observers to question UK claims to moral authority and civility. Also, if the 28-day limit were extended, Liberty concludes, might not some other states 'see this as a green light for them to take more severe action against groups and individuals they consider a threat'?

There is an important point worth making about other lands and procedures for making charges and ordering detention. No two legal systems are exactly the same and to draw valid comparisons is difficult. The UK Common Law system underlies legal systems in Canada, Australia, New Zealand and Eire. In Europe, however, some countries like France, Italy, Germany and Spain have inquisitorial Civil Law systems, without a concept of pre-charge detention as the United Kingdom has in practice. On the other hand, maximum periods for stipulated terrorist offences are carefully observed and regulated in Italy, France, Spain, Germany,

Denmark, Norway, Russia and Turkey. There, any police request for extra questioning time will be examined by senior judicial staff. In certain other states there is no sign at the moment that police and security authorities in any way see present detention limits as inadequate and hampering investigation.

There is nothing like so much concern about suspects' detention in the United States as there is in the United Kingdom. The permitted length of detention remains at two days, with the proviso that an extension can be applied for by the security services. Most of the public debate centres around the reported ill-treatment of detainees before they are sent to further imprisonment. There is a great deal of speculation and argument about the extent to which interrogation methods resort to inhuman manipulation. Suspects on release have been reluctant to go into detail. Media sources have been less restrained in their comments and questions. Solitary confinement is everywhere the rule. Is not waterboarding used here and there? The US Vice-President, Dick Cheney, no less, is said to have defended that practice specifically. In October 2007, *The New York Times* gave the Administration as finding it difficult to turn away critics of something authorised at high level, something referred to as 'enhanced interrogation' techniques. Conversations with CIA interrogators on television programmes were lifting the curtain on information, formerly classified, that divulged 'hard measures for hard characters'. Valuable information had been gained but at what cost? Coercion, it was supposed, had 'opened the dialogue'. Quite possibly, now and at last, detainees are benefiting from a scaling back of interrogation practices now that so much has been brought out into the open.

On 10 March 2008 *The Times* reported a collision course with Congress in Washington where President George Bush was wielding a rare presidential veto to block legislation banning the CIA from applying force in interrogating terrorist suspects. The President was set to upend a bill from the Democrats that would limit the CIA to a range of methods approved by the US Army. An Army manual lists 19 means of interrogation and specifically rules out coercive techniques such as the simulated drowning of water-boarding. Presidential intentions were made clear to Congress. 'This is not the time,' he said 'to abandon practices that have a proven track record of keeping America safe.' Any attempt to weaken CIA interrogators must weaken them in the fight against al-Qaida. Moreover, there was some White House support for director of the CIA, Mike Hayden, who approved the Bush veto and went on to brush aside anxieties in the Justice Department and the Pentagon. Hayden argued that Army practice was inappropriate as a guide for the CIA. Different missions, different capabilities and, therefore, differences in procedure characterised the CIA and the Army institutions. Against the view from the top, Democrat and Republican Congressmen have not found it at all easy to get violation of human rights the prominence and publicity it deserves. Democrats attempted to overturn the veto but Congress sustained it in March 2008.

Imprisonment

The debate and the protest over detention policies in the United Kingdom and the United States are miniscule compared with the outrage, mainly in the Western world, that erupts whenever Guantanamo Bay is mentioned. On account of media coverage, that name is synonymous with a secretive punishment regime that secludes terrorist suspects for years at a time, that is reputed to treat them inhumanely and where there appears to be scant concern for charge, trial, appeal and eventual release. Secrecy masks much of what happens in Guantanamo Bay prison on the island of Cuba. Not much is known about investigation procedures there and ways in which charge and trial are managed by its military commissions (tribunals). What is known is that such commissions act most unconventionally. 'Sensitive' evidence may be withheld by the defence, indefinite detention without trial is allowable, conviction may be based on hearsay, there is no recourse to other courts and due process and any appeal would have to go to the President who jammed the suspect in the first place.

A certain number of facts have been brought out by released prisoners and official visitors. Even a brief recapitulation of circumstances makes for agonised listening in the view of those who have encountered it. Guantanamo Bay detention camp was established as a naval base for the United States on a perpetual lease before the days of Fidel Castro, then run down in the 1970s, to be reopened as a holding facility for Cuban and Haitian refugees. As a detention centre the place has been operational since April 2002. Much of the security force there is US military police. Their watch is over inmates accused by the US Government of being potential terrorists as well as those treated as suspects who are being held pending relocation elsewhere. The term 'suspect' is, of course, very much an arguable concept. An illustration of this is, again in press reporting, that US Army data on 517 detainees, when analysed, shows only 8 per cent accused of association with al-Qaida, and fewer than half charged with ever having been involved in any activity hostile to the United States. Who are the terrorist suspects? Many of them are probably hapless Afghans caught up in the sweeping confusions of life in their country; some, indeed, are supportive of the Taliban resolve, others are from Jordan and Morocco, and may have been attracted to Kabul by the prospect of a new life under a truly Islamic regime.

Since the beginning of the war in Afghanistan, 775 detainees have been brought to Guantanamo, approximately 420 of whom have been released. At the moment something of the order of 400 remain. Although new blocks have been built to accommodate a possible 2,000, more than a fifth of these have been cleared for release but they may have to wait months or years, since US officials do not easily find relocation for those freed. It is never straightforward ascertaining precise numbers but US officials say they intend eventually to put at least 80 detainees on trial and free the rest. A major complexity is that the United States has to negotiate with 43 or so countries to finalise arrangements for detainee release. Currently, there appear to be nationals from Saudi Arabia, Yemen, Pakistan, India, Afghanistan, Iraq, Iran, Algeria and Syria, with small numbers from the United Kingdom. A fair number of these suspects are being 'rendered' on to other countries under 'rendition' programmes, as we shall see in Chapter 9.

Something that has grievously complicated the whole picture is the actual status in law of these detainees. What might be termed international haggling has gone on since the camp's inception in 2002. Washington has classified detainees as 'enemy combatants' rather than as prisoners of war. This is stated to be in line with Article 4 of the Geneva Convention on Human Rights. Following definition in that Article, the Government points out that the detainees have neither the status of civilians, nor of regular soldiers, nor of guerillas or militia. They are not enlisted soldiers of a recognised government. The 'laws and customs of war' do not apply to them, but there is no intermediate status: nobody can be outside the law. Also, under the Geneva Convention, a detainee may seek to demonstrate that the factual circumstances of his arrest may have been misleading (e.g. arrest of an apparent 'terrorist') and that he is not a member of a hostile fighting force at all. A complicating argument, something of a circular one legally, is that the detainees are seen as criminals by the United States, where criminal law (with its constitutional protections) does not apply because they are 'enemy combatants'. Another term frequently applied to the detainee is 'alien' and that is contestable in law, especially when it is derogatory. This sort of arbitrary classification is not at all acceptable to the International Committee of the Red Cross, or to the UN. The designation of 'enemy combatants' not only cuts across international law but it has consigned between 500 and 600 detainees to a vacuum lacking law and careful supervision. Recent US court rulings are no help to most detainees.

Angela Merkel, Germany's Chancellor, has lately condemned the forms of 'torture' used in the infamous camp. Britain's Prime Minister, Tony Blair, shortly before his resignation in 2007, declared Guantanamo 'an anomaly and sooner or later it's got to be dealt with'. Cabinet colleagues of his branded the Cuban centre as 'unacceptable', tarnishing US traditions of liberty and justice and altogether 'a shocking affront to democracy'. Lower echelon representatives in government, members of secular and religions organisations all the time express amazement that a civilised world cannot force Washington to close Guantanamo for good. UK critics in particular believe their national government is acting tamely, if not hypocritically, in not pressing the United States to do what it should, both morally and legally. There are some signs of this message getting home. On 21 December 2007, the US Secretary of State, Condoleezza Rice, reiterated what she declared was the desire of the President to help close the camp as soon as possible. She indicated that the only problem remaining was that of seeking guarantees from nations whose national detainees would be a danger on their release.

Will Guantanamo close its doors in 2009? Irene Khan, head of Amnesty International, is hopeful. She has christened this appalling place 'the gulag of our time'. There they have no law and no rights. There is, according to Khan, a realisation among US policymakers that the Cuban jail is a tremendous liability.

People, Khan believes, do not have to be locked up forever. For realists there must be an alternative. An exit strategy, fair and workable, has to be searched for.

A recent detainee in Guantanamo, Moazzam Begg, acquired a wide public profile, in the spring of 2008. His book *Enemy*

Combatant and numerous appearances at human rights campaign meetings and on TV tell a horrifying story. A Muslim born in Birmingham, he was one of the nine British detainees. His spell of incarceration lasted three years, much of it shackled and in solitary confinement. With legal and social work experience, he had been assisting relief operations in Afghanistan and Bosnia when he was 'snatched' by a Pakistan intelligence squad in Kabul. US security was there, too, dressed in Pakistani attire. Handcuffed, he was accused of associating with Taliban adherents. Ultimately, by a circuitous route, Begg was 'rendered' to Cuba. Shortly after his arrival, he was asked to sign a six-page 'confession' which his captors had fashioned. Occasionally there was a contact with Begg's homeland, inquisitorial visits from British consular staff and MI5.

Some six months later the possibility of trial by military commission was raised. Begg did not relish the outcome of a secretive grilling, without a jury or defence, by a uniformed representative of those who had labelled him 'terrorist'. More time elapsed until Guantanamo began to experiment with Combatant Status Review Tribunals, probably as some sort of concession to the gale of condemnation from across the world. The Supreme Court in Washington and other courts were now facing up to the notions of release and eventual camp closure, despite the obduracy of the White House. Release did come at last without any explanation or apology.

Belmarsh Prison

'A Guantanamo in our own back yard', is the view of Liberty, condemning the state of things in Belmarsh Prison, Woolwich, south-east London. 'The similarities are striking and appalling. The lack of rights afforded to men in both prisons undermines the concept of fundamental civil liberties.' Amnesty International concurs:

The men are held in small cells for 22 hours a day. How is that proper treatment? We have heard reports of inadequate health care, restricted access to legal advice, to the outside world and to the practicing of their religion. The conditions are cruel, inhuman and degrading. The parallels with Guantanamo Bay are stark.

In December 2001, nine foreign nationals were taken by police from their families and brought to Belmarsh Prison. No explanations from their captives were sufficient to get the picture clear. They were clearly suspected of something. The detainees were unable to see any incriminating evidence nor were they able to have full discussions with solicitors, who reckoned the detainees were 'entombed in concrete'. Non-English speakers found it particularly difficult to make any sense of their plight since interpreters were not readily present nor was any form of social worker available. In 2006 Belmarsh was holding 900 men, 10 per cent of them Muslims. All were being held on charges represented by the Anti-terrorism, Crime and Security Act of December 2001. High-profile terrorist suspects were kept separate in a high-security prison within a prison. These were considered 'exceptional risk' prisoners. Conditions in a prison now at 'full stretch' were not at all good was the admission of Anne Owers, the Chief Inspector of Prisons, in 2006. There was evidence of bullying and of lack of consideration by staff for prisoners' need for exercise and social contact in a multi-cultural environment. She said that prison staff did not understand the social and religious behaviour and interactions of Muslims, in spite of the efforts of a collaborative and trusted imam. It was vital for prison officers to understand their Muslim inmates and the different relationships with and between them in order to manage them safely. There were 17 religious faiths being practised in Belmarsh. Four remand prisoners on terror charges, she added, were only allowed to associate in pairs and were banned from their Friday communal prayers. As some concession to prisoner needs Muslims are allowed their imams working in a multi-faith chaplaincy team. Yet, such is the diversity of faiths and cultural origins that prison staff find the supervision of their charges very demanding and unpredictable.

Something else problematic to deal with is the possible radical-isation of prisoners by terrorist extremists. The influx of many hardened terrorists into prisons has begun to worry the Home Office because of their likely destructive impact and the potential for susceptible, imprisoned youths to be influenced by high-profile terrorist suspects. Prison officers remember the days of the Irish Troubles of the 1970s–80s when prisons became rallying points for the IRA. The Vice-Chairman of the Prison Officers Association, Steve Gough, put it candidly: 'The majority of the prison population is composed of angry young men, disenfran-chised from society, it doesn't matter if they are English, Afro-Caribbean or whatever. These people are ripe for radicalisation'. One solution to this, which is being tried, is the dispersal around the nation's prisons of those charged with terrorist offences. Concern remains, although the Ministry of Justice and the Home Office are holding urgent talks about it.

Public pressure has led the UK Government to urge the United States to give the British prisoners in Guantanamo a fair trial. In the case of Belmarsh inmates, nothing much happened before 2004 to alleviate their being held for up to three years before being brought before any court. Parliament was ready in December 2003 to take the problem in hand. The Newton Committee, made up of senior MPs and peers, all privy coun-sellors, and chaired by a Conservative, Lord Newton, were sharply critical of the Belmarsh system. 'Powers which allow foreign nationals to be detained potentially indefinitely should be replaced as a matter of urgency.' It was not at all clear that gov-ernment policy made Britain a safer place, perhaps not so. There was understandable disquiet among the Muslim population about indefinite detention.

Further consideration of the Belmarsh system took place in October 2004 with the convening of a special House of Lords

Judicial Committee who appointed nine judges to examine the case for indefinite prison holding without charge or trial. Their case was in regard to a Court of Appeal decision in October 2002 which held that indefinite detention was compatible with UK and international law. This decision (occasioning much public consternation) reversed a July 2002 ruling from the Special Immigration Appeals Commission that the Government's powers were discriminatory and in breach of the United Kingdom's obligations under human rights laws. Controversy about the Belmarsh system, and more widely about the UK Government's policies as to indefinite detention continues vigorously. Most of those in the debate share the view of the Newton Committee that conventional criminal prosecution procedures are the most effective way forward. The usual, fair-trial safeguards must be observed. Where there are obstacles to unqualified observance of human rights, then law reforms will be necessary. Certainly, there are signs that the treatment of Belmarsh prisoners, and crucially their position in law, is receiving focused attention in Whitehall.

The entire scenario of dealing with terrorist suspects makes for neglect, uncertainty and contradiction – their arrest, their detention, the incoherence behind charging them, their imprisonment, the appeals and the government and judicial decisions. Questions are there by the hundred. One rights worker in the United States has put it baldly: 'treating those detainees living in a limbo – it's all of a helter-skelter game – messing about with to and fro legislation'. There is everything perhaps in the question voiced by a Guantanamo British detainee: 'if you were not a terrorist when you came here, won't you be one by the time you leave?'

Postscript

The long-term controversy over the UK Government's bill to extend detention from 28 to 42 days provided an interesting development in the last days of April 2008. On Wednesday 28 April, the Director of Public Prosecutions, Sir Ken Macdonald, told a committee meeting in Parliament to consider the proposed extension, that there was no need to change the current 28-day limit. He continued:

For our part as prosecutors . . . [w]e don't perceive any need for the period of 28 days to be increased. Our experience has been that we have managed quite comfortably within 28 days. We have therefore not asked for an increase to 28 days. It is possible to set up all sorts of hypotheses . . . Anything is possible – the question is whether it is remotely likely.

He believed that prosecutors were 'better placed' than the police to judge whether or not there was enough evidence for a suspect to be charged. His opinion was supported by Sue Hemming, Head of the Crown Prosecution Service Counter-terrorism Division, who told the committee that suspension for more than 14 days had only been needed on three occasions since the 28-day limit had been introduced in 2005.

Macdonald was accompanied by former Attorney-General, Lord Goldsmith, who was equally forthright:

The case has not been made out for that extension, and I can't possibly support it. It is also counter-productive, because it sends a message to particularly the Muslim communities that we are down on them, and misguided young men might take it as justification for taking up arms, as they see it, against us. We have had and the police have had significant plots to investigate. But in none of those cases, and I looked hard at them when I was in government, would it have been of help to have a period of longer than 28 days.

Meanwhile, the Metropolitan Police Commissioner and the Home Secretary have not relinquished their campaign to see extension granted. They and everybody else will now have to consider a change in law materially affecting the issue of extension. The threshold of evidence needed to bring charges in serious cases is now lower. Crucially, this now means that a suspect may be charged if there is 'reasonable suspicion' that they may be guilty of a crime rather than the full requirement of 'a realistic prospect of conviction'. An early opinion about this change is that of Lord Falconer, former Lord Chancellor, who argues that 'the debate about should it be 28 days, 42 days or 90 days has moved on because of the threshold standard'. Changes such as this may not be easy for some resolute protagonists to accept. Is it not all of a piece with the obvious fact that counter-terrorism proposal and practice are changing all the time beneath our feet, and helpfully so?

9

Rendition: kidnapping suspects by order

'Rendition' is a comparatively new word. It crops up now almost every day in newspapers and on radio. The term describes something to do with counter-terrorism that is illegal, largely inhuman and, frankly, bizarre. In so many respects it is unfathomable yet widely practised. Those governments which have a hand in it, either brazenly or covertly, do not like to be approached about it. Altogether, then, this makes for surmise, enquiry, protest and revulsion. This is the stuff of great debate and already there is vociferous clamour for action.

Definition and scale

Amnesty International for some years has subjected rendition to minute and very wide scrutiny. It put out a plain definition of rendition as:

The transfer of individuals from one country to another, by means that bypass all judicial and administrative due process. In the 'war on terror' context, the practice is mainly – although not exclusively – initiated by the USA, and carried on with the collaboration, complicity, or acquiescence of other governments. The most widely known manifestation of rendition is the secret transfer of terror subjects into the custody of other states – including, Jordan and Syria – where physical and psychological brutality features prominently in interrogations. The rendition networks' aim is to use whatever means necessary to gather intelligence, and to keep detainees away from any judicial oversight.

> The network also is used to transfer people into US custody, where they may end up in Guantanamo Bay, Iraq or Afghanistan, or in secret facilities known as 'black sites' run by the CIA. In some cases, detainees have been moved in and out of US custody several times. Rendition, as a form of official kidnapping or organised 'disappearance', is designed to dodge judicial and public scrutiny, to disguise the identity of the organisers and to conceal the fate of victims. Certainly, the practice deserves its connotation, now accepted by government and critic, of 'extra-ordinary rendition' (something extraordinary to the law and extraordinary in going beyond easy credibility). A variant of this is 'irregular rendition'. Some critics use the term 'torture by proxy' to refer to situations in which the United States has straight-forwardly transferred suspected terrorists to countries known to rely on harsh interrogation methods, including forms of torture.

> Occasionally, rendition organisers attempt to present it as an efficient way of transferring terrorist suspects from place to place with the minimum of red tape. Such a claim evades the truth that the system places the victim outside the protection of the law and gives the perpetrator the licence to ignore legality. Quite clearly, rendition involves multiple violations of human rights. Victims have been originally arrested and detained peremptorily and illegally, most of them denied access to any legal process, particularly the chance to challenge arbitrary decisions. The threat of ill-treatment and torture is always there.

> Secrecy masks any attempt to estimate the scope of what is 'enforced disappearance'. Understandably, detainees' families may be reluctant to report their relatives as missing, in the fear that the CIA may turn upon them. Occasionally, a released detainee contacts the media and there is every indication that the number of cases of unlawful abduction now runs into

hundreds. There is every scope for mistakes in arrests now known to governments and to critics as 'erroneous rendition', where an innocent person is detained because of misinterpreted behaviour or posture, or even silence when questioned. Security personnel may confuse names and identity or fail to understand language or accent.

A great deal of the criticism of rendition centres on the 'rendering' or transportation of detainees to countries that are notorious for ill-treating prisoners, countries such as Egypt, Syria, Morocco and Jordan. The whereabouts and conditions of most rendition victims remain hidden, so that precise circumstances are not easy to ascertain. What is in no doubt is the absolute obligation not to extradite any person to a country where they risk torture (the principle of non-refoulement). This principle is a cardinal feature of the International Convention Against Torture adopted by the UN General Assembly in 1984, which subsequently 141 nations have ratified. In acceding to the Convention governments must observe non-refoulement, investigate all allegations of torture and provide a remedy to identified victims. Even if a person is suspected of having committed a terrorist act, it is illegal to send them to any place where there is a chance of torture. Governments are anxious not to be seen as transgressors of a humane principle. Yet, transfers may go through since governments argue that their own first obligation is not to provide a safe harbour for the terrorist. The American Secretary of State, Condoleezza Rice, in a radio interview in April 2006 insisted that her country has never transported anyone to a land known for its inhumane methods of getting information. Statements in Congress and from the US Department of Justice have reaffirmed this position. Facts, however, speak otherwise. In an attempt at least to stand by the Convention, states have devised a reliance on 'diplomatic assurances', where a state seeking to transfer somebody seeks assurance that the receiving state is not going to carry out any form of torture or inhumane treatment. Most states asked to provide such a guarantee have already signed binding legal conventions prohibiting malpractice, and have ignored them. One or two questions can be asked here. First, if the risk of torture in custody is so significant that assurances have to be sought, is any permitted transfer feasible? Second, does not recourse to diplomatic assurances create a situation where neither state has an interest in monitoring agreement effectively, since any breach of the agreement implicates both in internationally forbidden acts? There is little doubt that some countries providing diplomatic assurances deny that torture exists there despite what is well known about routine practices. An interesting illustration of states' dilemmas over these assurances came to light in London in April 2008. The UK Government sought to deport three terrorist suspects, two Libyans and one Jordanian, back to their home countries. Assurances dubbed 'memorandums of understanding' had been received from Jordan and Libya promising that the returnees would not be maltreated on arrival. The proposal to deport went before an immigration appeals commission in London who ruled that the Government would rely on diplomatic assurances. Not so was the opinion of three Appeal Court judges in blocking the deportation orders. There was, in fact, no absolute guarantee either of humane treatment or a fair trial in Libya or Jordan. Amnesty International lost no time in calling on London to abandon such unassured deportations.

The terms 'guarantee' and 'understanding' raise key issues relating to how far the 'renderer' appreciates what may happen to the individual 'rendered'. Quite recently the Law Society in Britain has pronounced on the matter. Their statement, given its importance to British service personnel, is worth quoting in full (as printed in *The Guardian* of 29 September 2008):

British troops who hand over prisoners in Iraq to US military personnel could find themselves facing prosecution, according to a legal opinion compiled for parliament. The finding has led to calls for the British government to rethink its current policy and investigate how the US treats its prisoners, and whether torture is employed against them.

Earlier this year the all-party parliamentary group on extraordinary rendition sought legal opinion from Michael Fordham QC on whether a human rights violation would arise under the ECHR and the 1998 Human Rights Act (HRA) if an individual in British detention in Iraq were handed over to US military personnel, 'despite substantial grounds for considering that there is a real risk of that person being subjected to torture or inhuman and degrading treatment'.

The conclusion reached by Fordham and his colleague Tom Hickman is that an offence would definitely have been committed. If acted on, the opinion could mean that UK troops would not be allowed to 'render' detainees to the US military until it was clear that they would no longer face the possibility of torture or ill-treatment.

What prompted the inquiry was a statement made in February 2008 by Ben Griffin, a former SAS soldier who was on active service in Iraq. In his statement, Griffin said that he was 'in no doubt' that individuals handed over to the US military 'would be tortured'. He cited what had happened to those detained at Guantanamo Bay, Bagram airbase and Abu Ghraib Prison.

The opinion adds: 'UK forces operating in Iraq are potentially also subject to UK criminal law, tort law and Iraqi law. Notably, the Criminal Justice Act 1988 makes it a criminal offence for a public official, whatever his nationality and wherever located, to commit an act of torture'.

Andrew Tyrie, the Conservative MP who chairs the committee which commissioned the report, said there had been a number of allegations that UK forces had been capturing people and handing them over to US authorities, knowing that these detainees were at risk of being tortured or mistreated.

'I commissioned a legal opinion to establish whether the UK acted unlawfully when they were handed over', said Tyrie. 'I now have the answer. The UK remains legally responsible for the subsequent treatment of anybody who has been detained by the UK. It is likely that British policy on this area is not only ethically questionable but is also unlawful. The government now needs to radically rethink its policy on this issue.'

Clive Stafford Smith, director of the legal action charity Reprieve, also welcomed the findings. 'We are delighted that the all-party parliamentary group has recognised the illegality of British troops handing over prisoners to US custody in Iraq', he said. 'These prisoners promptly disappear into an unaccountable prison network in which over 20,000 prisoners are held for illegal interrogation and torture. If it is confirmed that this has been happening, the British government must immediately reveal how many people have been handed over, where they are now, and what has been done to them.'

Paul Marsh, president of the Law Society, called on the Government to investigate what happens to prisoners rendered from British custody. 'Extraordinary rendition has been used by some states as a means of bypassing the formal justice system', said Marsh. 'To do so is a breach of the rule of law and puts individuals at risk of ill-treatment. The Law Society calls on the UK government to look beyond assurances from other countries and positively investigate and monitor whether individuals rendered from British custody are receiving equivalent standards of due process. It is time we returned to our values in the rule of law.'

The United States and rendition

Before September 2001 and 9/11 rendition was mainly conceived of as a way of returning terrorism suspects to the United States for trial. On 1 June 1995 President Bill Clinton issued a Presidential Decision in the following words:

When terrorists wanted for violation of US law are at large overseas, their return for prosecution shall be a matter of the highest priority . . . If we do not receive adequate cooperation from a state that harbors a terrorist whose extradition we are seeking, we shall take appropriate measures to induce cooperation . . .

Less brusque in address, directives of a similar nature were issued from the Bush presidency in 1992: the contents remain classified. It was September 1998 that the FBI Director testified to ongoing concern:

During the past decade the United States has successfully returned 13 suspected terrorists to stand trial in the United States for acts or planned acts of terrorism against US citizens. Based on its policy of treating terrorists as criminals and applying the rule of law against them, the United States is one of the most visible and effective forces in identifying, locating and apprehending terrorists on American soil and overseas . . .

About this time and in contrast, certain US agencies were arranging to 'render' terrorist suspects to third countries, where the intention was not that of trial but to keep them out of circulation and in custody and certainly without any access to US courts. A former CIA chief has revealed that their earlier programme to treat suspects as prisoners of war (with statutory rights) was nullified by the White House.

To get the guys off the streets was best even if Egypt, with its hard reputation, were the destination. Having failed to find a legal means to keep all the detainees in American custody, they preferred to let other countries do our dirty work . . .

Amnesty International has noted that publicly there was at first the description of rendition as a workable means of working with foreign governments to bring back suspects to US justice and trial. In 2004 Congress was told that rendition has netted 'many dozens of terrorists'. No trials were then mentioned: nor were the identity and the role of third-party receiver states made clear. Media reports increasingly referred to the plight of suspects arrested, blindfolded, shackled, sedated and transported in jump suits by private jet to covert imprisonment. Government spokesmen generally treated enquiry and protest tight lipped.

Once more, Amnesty International keeps close watch and reports. Clearly, since the trauma of 2001 the direction of rendition has been modified. Cofer Black, CIA Counter-terrorism Center Director until May 2002, is quoted describing the rendition programme as " 'No Limits', aggressive, relentless, worldwide pursuit of any terrorist who threatens us". Are basic human rights disposable then? Amnesty's view is that the aim now is to ensure that suspects are not brought to trial, rather, without any attempt to marshal pre-trial evidence, they must be handed over to foreign governments for interrogation ('extraordinary rendition') or impounded on 'black sites' under US Army guard. Significantly now, it is the CIA who directs the programme not inter-agency collaboration. Once more, it is 'hard measures for hard cases' and 'grab first, ask questions later'.

The practicalities of rendering suspects have been set down in detail by Amnesty International (on 5 April 2006 on their website). Even skeletal Amnesty records point to some 1,600 CIA rendition flights mainly via Europe. The devious ways in which international conventions and strict laws are circumvented by the CIA and, shamefully, by many governments is ludicrous, if it were not disgraceful and unethical. For instance, the so-called Chicago Convention on International Civil Aviation 1944, revised many times and adopted in 2000 with 189 contracting states, establishes rules for the use of airspace, aircraft registration and safety. Why, though, does a clause allow private, non-commercial flights to fly over a country or make technical stops there without prior notification and authorisation? Not surprisingly, the US military and intelligence branches have long used private air carriers for secret transportations operations. Masterminding these enterprises, the CIA devotes much time and effort to preventing outsiders tracking rendition flights. Notwithstanding their care (or cunning), rendition watchers have been able to log names of participating air companies, the number of flights of the 'ghost planes' and the airfields being used. Strangely, the FBI also carries out renditions and transports its suspects by US Air Force jet rather than private aircraft, a way of doing it which is not too difficult to track.

Is there no way, Conventions or otherwise, of the US rendition programme being halted or progressively downscaled? In fact the Chicago Convention does provide for required on-transit landing of an aircraft if there are 'reasonable grounds to conclude that it is being used for any purpose inconsistent with the aims of the Convention'. Is not the violation of international law, the ignoring of Convention safety and passenger stipulations and the evasion of torture prohibition so clear in that required landings of aircraft suspected of rendition handling would be mandatory? That, at least, would be a start to bringing down an inhuman programme, backed by General Mike Hayden, the present CIA chief as 'a very controversial programme' yielding 'irreplaceable intelligence'. Some programme!

The United Kingdom and rendition

How could our Government ever get mixed up in something so unethical and law-breaking? How could they? How could they not see that the idea and the programme denied some people their basic human rights? This sort of question is frequently heard these days. Indeed, how could a modern government, instantly informed and always ready to respond to circumstances, play any sort of part in an affair internationally regarded as unsupportable? It should matter that those who criticise and reject the rendition programme are politicians of every persuasion, lawyers, academics, media people, religious leaders and a host of concerned members of the public.

It certainly does not help critic or government spokesperson that what 'Authority' puts about in answer to query is generally sketchy, controversial and, sometimes, contradictory. Shortness of official detail obviously fuels speculation. The years 2005 and

2006, in particular, were years in which the press carried out surveys and in which Whitehall's stance was neither to refute nor adequately to explain. In December 2005, the House of Commons Foreign Affairs Committee was minded to open its own investigations. 'We are actively pursuing it; we are not letting it drop', they said.

Also in December 2005, *The Guardian* launched the first of a number of press surveys of rendition. The CIA, they found, was using 19 UK airports for a 26-strong fleet of mainly private US jet aircraft, which had made short refuelling stops, occasionally stopping for longer. Since 2001, there had been 210 flights in and out of the country on a weekly basis. The favourite touchdown was Prestwick in Scotland. Were detainees on board to be ferried on to devious locations? There is no incontrovertible evidence that any terrorist suspects were on board. The aircraft might have been carrying personnel associated with the rendition scheme. Nor is there any suggestion that any of the UK airport authorities had colluded in any wrongdoing. *The Guardian* left the situation as problematic, with every possibility of a 'strong probability' of some rendition link-up. Almost certainly, given the reported destinations of the aircraft and, indeed, the air of incoherence, there was something unusual and mysterious in these aircraft movements. What continues to worry most observers is the lack of firm reply from Government. Were not airport officials and Foreign Office representatives asking the questions as to flight purpose, destinations and routes?

Lawyers' questions and frequent recriminations about rendition continue to rumble. There is still, in some legal chambers, astonishment about the Foreign Office declaration in March 2003 that it was not illegal under the UN Convention Against Torture for the United Kingdom to obtain or use intelligence gained under torture, provided that the United Kingdom itself did not employ torture or request that a named individual be tortured. Was this not disingenuous in the extreme? This position was confirmed by a unanimous Law Lords judgement on 8 December 2005. Under UK law tradition, information extracted by 'torture and its fruits' were unusable in court. However, the material thus acquired could be used by UK police and security services, as 'it would be ludicrous for them to disregard information about a ticking bomb even if it had been procured by torture'. To the strong dismay of human rights activists the Law Lords dismissed concern about the validity of information secured under duress.

Controversy was to flare up in February 2008, when David Milliband, the British Foreign Secretary, had to reveal that the Indian Ocean island of Diego Garcia, nominally a British territory, was used as a refuelling stop for at least two obvious rendition flights in 2002. Embarrassingly, Milliband had to admit that London had only just learned of this from Washington. Extraordinary rendition had been a consequence of extraordinary omission. Henceforth, the United Kingdom must have 'specific assurances' on all flights where concerns had been expressed regarding the use of British territory. Both flights had only a single detainee aboard, neither left the aircraft and neither was a British subject. Giving rise to parliamentary consternation was the understanding that one flight was bound for Cuba's Guantanamo, the other to the doubtful locale of Morocco. Also, while the Union Jack waved over the island some 3,000 US service personnel were responsible for the island's security. The US base camp had an ironical name: Camp Justice.

A combination, perhaps, of public pressure and 'lateness' in government disclosure will almost certainly move Whitehall to investigate alleged US misconduct within the United Kingdom's jurisdiction, that is, at airports and in places like Diego Garcia. A policy of non-compliance with the demands or requests from any other state to assist with such a programme as rendition must be put in place. Collaboration with other EU Member States should see the matter of violation of rights referred to the European Court of Human Rights.

Europe and rendition

'Condi upsets the pot' – this was how, on 6 December 2005, *The Sun* described a week's visit to Europe by Condoleezza Rice, the US Secretary of State. What was planned as an amicable exploration of trans-Atlantic relationships including discussion of counter-terrorism turned out to be a welter of public argument, some of it quite hostile. What occasioned the welter was the headlining of rendition, originally in *The Washington Post* and then across many of Europe's broadsheets and in radio commentaries.

Dr Rice handled her questioners with aplomb. There was no alternative to candid admission of a rendition operation across the Atlantic into Europe and beyond. Detainee flights were saving lives. They were a powerful tool in the war on terror for the United States and its allies. Movements such as these were permissible under international law, she stated bravely to an obviously ruffled audience in Berlin. Never would Washington countenance torture. More positively, the point was made that European cooperation with the United States was 'a two-way street' where her country had respected the sovereignty of other nations. Trust and cooperation were vital – we were all in the same boat. How was it, then, that *The Washington Post* and other sources were talking about the shadowy 'black sites' prisons in Romania and Poland (countries she was soon to visit)? Was it so because a number of European governments, one of them Germany, had connived in some of the CIA's murkier operations?

Had there not been, according to *Der Spiegel*, over 400 suspicions flights into German airfields alone? No comment, save, 'Were I to confirm or deny, say yes or say no, then I would be compromising intelligence information, and I am not going to do that', Rice added. Members of the Berlin photo-opportunity were too polite to slow handclap; the press in many lands were less restrained. The stand-up robustness of Rice was commended, even though the discerning might find double meaning and possibly evasion in what she said. What, after all, can one make of her seeing rendition as 'not unique to the United States, nor to the current administration' and, more questionably, her point that 'the captured terrorists of the twenty-first century do not fit easily into the traditional systems of criminal or military justice'?

The pot of public opinion was certainly near boiling point, it was a case of whether or not it was to be upset. There seemed little point in berating Rice, cool and finely informed. Other issues were to stem from Washington's devising of a programme, its confirmation and expansion, its refusal to recognise and remove the political, public and ethical failings. In short, there was gross violation of fundamental rights. How far were European administrations and security services in the know? Could it have been so that some European governments would not have pushed Dr Rice too hard for fear of embarrassing themselves as well as her? In December 2005, it was becoming plain that, even though conspiracy might put up a wall of silence, the riddle of rendition would have the European Commission, the Council of Europe, the EU, national parliaments, the UN, human rights groups and the world's media all launching enquiries and continuing to demand answers.

From logistics to turning a blind eye

Another quotation, this time from *The Guardian* of 7 June 2006, showed that Europe as a businesslike entity was moving into enquiry and demand. Back in November 2005, some weeks before the Rice visits, the Council of Europe instructed Dick Marty to institute a comprehensive survey and report on rendition and Europe. Marty, a Swiss lawyer, lost no time. On 25 November, he announced that latitude and longitude coordinates had been obtained for those East European 'black sites'. He planned to use satellite imagery over the last several years as part of his surveying. Three days later, and a most interesting coincidence, the European Union Justice and Home Affairs

Commissioner, Franco Frattini, threatened that any EU state operating a secret prison system would incur 'serious consequences', including the suspension of voting rights in the EU Council. At the same time, Brussels dispatched one of Frattini's senior colleagues to Washington to ask direct questions about the CIA prisons.

In time, Marty, having upset the pot, would table his report in Brussels. Meanwhile, a number of European governments were assembling their own data banks about rendition. In France, human rights groups were becoming insistent that Paris investigate a fair number of irregular flights by private aircraft whose registration numbers had been noted by plane-spotters. CIA sponsorship was suspected. Were detainees abroad? What did the French Government know about this? The outcome of all this was a display of magisterial silence-plus-readiness-to-inform that kept the ministries back-pedalling and the rights activists mystified and resentful. Spain's enquiry was more forceful and answered openly. In November 2005 *El Pais* ran an editorial reporting that two CIA planes had landed in the Canary Islands and in Palma de Mallorca. The flights were in 2003 and 2004 and had only just been discovered. An obliging Madrid attorney opened up an investigation. The flights, it seemed, had touched down in Baghdad and Afghanistan and then Poland, somewhat unconventional routes. The Spanish Civil Guard, also obligingly, offered to try to track the aircraft crews. Confronted in their hotels, American personnel were entirely silent about their flights, only confirming many suspicions about the origin and purpose of the flights.

German and Italian investigations mixed individual activists' insistence and a small degree of governmental clarification. Would Berlin be able to comment on reports that the CIA still uses an American military base to transport terrorism suspects without informing the German Government? There was, in November 2005, documentation of 85 take-offs and landings by aircraft with a 'high probability' of being operated by the CIA at Ramstein airfield. Berlin, always concerned about counter-terrorism, took its time on this occasion and replied that invest-igations were in hand. Italy's commendable speed in looking into rendition sparked a political furore. A radical Islamist imam, Hassan Nasr (or Abu Omar), was kidnapped in a joint CIA–Italian security corps snatch in Milan on 17 February 2007 and was rendered to Egypt, where he was to be held for four years. There, a Cairo court ruled imprisonment to be 'without foundation'. On his return from Egypt, Nasr convinced Rome that he had been tortured, both in Milan and Egypt. Italian prosecutors investigat-ing truly harsh and unjust treatment went on to indict 26 US citizens, including the director of the CIA in Italy and 24 other CIA agents. The security corps chief and his deputy were forced to resign on indictment.

An investigation of rendition by Portugal in February 2007 also brought political controversy in its train. Two Socialist Members of the European Parliament, themselves from Spain, had called upon Lisbon to look into the matter of 'illegal activities and seri-ous human rights violations'. This was done, although one of the Members rebuked Portugal's Foreign Minister for delay in open-ing the search and publicly remarked that she was convinced that two successive governments over the period 2002 to 2005 had given the CIA permission for the operation of 24 or so flights.

At last, on 7 June 2006, the conclusive report on rendition came from Dick Marty, now chair of the Council of Europe Committee on Legal Affairs and Human Rights. The title was *Alleged Secret Detentions and Unlawful Inter-state Transfers Involving Council of Europe Member States*. With such a title, it is not surprising that it was received throughout Europe with tremendous anticipation and interest. After all, were not certain report conclusions rather breathtaking?

While the states of the Old World have dealt with these threats primarily by means of existing institutions and legal systems, the United States appears to have made a fundamentally different choice; considering that neither conventionally judicial instruments nor those established under the framework of the laws of war could effectively counter the new forms of international terrorism, it decided to develop new legal concepts. This legal approach is utterly alien to the European tradition and sensibility, and is clearly contrary to the European Convention on Human Rights and the universal Declaration of Human Rights.

This represented a rather sweeping opinion for European governments to consider. Marty took up the conjectures about the so-called 'black sites' and the likely complicity of certain East European states:

The compilation of so-called 'black lists' of individuals and companies suspected of maintaining connections with organisations considered terrorist and the application of the associated sanctions clearly breaches every principle of the fundamental right to a fair trial: no specific charges, no right to be heard, no right of appeal, no established procedure from removing one's names from the list.

Here the wording is a little debatable but the thrust of meaning was clear enough.

Something had to be done in Europe's capitals, and urgently. In June 2006, the same month as the report, the Council of Europe framed resolutions insisting on review of bilateral agreements between the United States and Council of Europe Member States 'to ensure they conform to international human rights norms'. In particular, the system of secret detentions and unlawful inter-state transfers must be dismantled. Prosecution of suspected terrorists should be regularised with, say, referral to the International Criminal Court. Those found to be implicated in rendition arrangements should also be considered indictable. A fresh global initiative to address the terrorist threat conforming again to democracy, human rights and the rule was imperative.

Eight months later, in February 2007, the European Parliament listed a number of states judged as tolerating something like

1,200 illegal CIA flights. They included Austria, Belgium, Cyprus, Denmark, Germany, Greece, Ireland, Italy, Poland, Portugal, Romania, Spain, Sweden and the United Kingdom. There was apparently wholesale unwillingness to cooperate. Marty's survey of 'the rendition circuit' certainly moved a logistical survey into the ifs-and-buts of deliberate governmental turning a blind eye. Red faces were to be expected. What it was now necessary to do was to uproot the rendition programmes and move into united state action.

Rendition; fact and fiction

What remains arguable is the extent to which public protest about something demonstrably bad shifts politicians. There is documentation from reputable high-level sources. Facts are clear. Most governments will not 'come clean'. In 2007 a fictional treatment of rendition was attempted by a British film company and screened worldwide. The film plot was modelled on actual stories of 'rendered' ones. Egyptian-born Anwar El-Ibrahim, living unremarkably in the United States, has a phone call from a person the CIA has logged as a suspected terrorist. Actually, the call is a social one and so really inconsequential. Not so in the eyes of the CIA. Anwar is kidnapped and 'disappeared' away to Morocco. A distraught wife cannot find out anything about her husband's fate. In Morocco Anwar, virtually in chains, is being 'encouraged' to cooperate and a torture regime is graphically enacted. Somewhat unexpectedly a CIA analyst, assigned to the prisoner's interrogation, handles the case gently since he grows convinced of Anwar's innocence. Indeed, he helps his interviewee to make an escape to safety in Spain, Anwar is able to return to the United States and is reunited with friends and family.

Facts are disturbingly presented in the film *Rendition* in fiction mode. Do they then provoke an audience into sad outrage? Do the stalls empty out observers now determined to show their disgust and ready to round on the CIA? Critics in the main thought the film worth doing as tough commentary on an unacceptable, inhumane situation. More than one critic appreciated the candour of showing what was 'right' and obviously 'wrong', though a caustic view was that the film was 'bust as a persuasive drama'. At any rate, the film, if not quite spurring viewers into action, has led to some wide discussion, surely, the beginnings of action.

Amnesty International's recommendations

In April 2006 Amnesty International published a strong, very comprehensive set of recommendations about the place of rendition in counter-terrorism, addressed to all governments. At the risk of duplication their most helpful, clear thinking is set out below in full:

No renditions

Do not render or otherwise transfer to the custody of another state anyone suspected or accused of security offences unless the transfer is carried out under judicial supervision and in full observance of due legal process.

Ensure that anyone subject to transfer has the right to challenge its legality before an independent tribunal, and that they have access to an independent lawyer and an effective right of appeal.

Do not receive into custody anyone suspected or accused of security offences unless the transfer is carried out under judicial supervision and in full observance of due legal process.

Information on the numbers, nationalities and current whereabouts of all terror suspects rendered, extradited, or otherwise transferred into custody from abroad should be publicly available. Full personal details should be promptly supplied to the families and lawyers of the detainees and to the International Committee of the Red Cross (ICRC).

Bring all such detainees before a judicial authority within 24 hours of entry into custody.

Ensure that detainees have prompt access to legal counsel and to family members, and that lawyers and family members are kept informed of the detainee's whereabouts.

Ensure that detainees who are not nationals of the detaining country have access to diplomatic or other representatives of their country of nationality or former habitual residence.

No 'disappearances', no secret detention.

End immediately the practices of incommunicado and secret detention wherever and under whatever agency it occurs.

Hold detainees only in officially recognised places of detention with access to family, legal counsel and courts.

Ensure that those responsible for 'disappearances' are brought to justice, and that victims and families receive restitution, compensation and rehabilitation.

Investigate any allegations that their territory hosts or has hosted secret detention facilities, and make public the results of such investigations.

The past, the present, the future

Those who have had some communication with government from time to time know only too well the need to climb mountains where officialdom receives, notes, routinely thanks, promises to consider and eventually arranges to get in touch. Directing a set of recommendations at any array of governments requires, in this instance, a careful acquaintance with the appropriateness of channels and people. It is useful to have an inexhaustible degree of patience to deal with their protocols and priorities. Rarely is it possible to predict how a chancellery will react to suggestions deemed 'essential and immediate steps' that are handed in from outside. Amnesty International's fine ideas would bring about a need for extensive review and replacement of the entrenched, CIA way of business, that is, the matters of arrest, categorisation, detention, transfer and imprisonment.

Presumably Amnesty sees it more comprehensively done through an international interface with sufficient authority and power to deal with governments, legislatures and security services. There would be the task of finding agreement on how states go about setting up adequate 'judicial supervision' and the ensuring of 'due legal process'. The definition of 'suspect terrorist activities and offences', unhelpfully variable and incoherent at the moment, would need mammoth efforts to achieve unison.

We can be hopeful that Europe's governments and the United States will find recommendations being seriously considered and not by foreign offices who see in earnest moves for rights an acknowledgement of what one critic made of the film *Rendition* – 'there's decency in this, but also a naivety and a moral equivalence . . .'.

Decency, yes, morality certainly. And how many lives are likely to be in peril?

Final thoughts – and the future?

Sixty years ago Eleanor Roosevelt surely expressed the hopes of a war-weary Europe and America that man's elemental rights could be encoded, proclaimed and implemented. It was, indeed, a 'breathless' world in her view full of expectations and resolve. There were to follow a Universal Declaration, Covenants, Conventions, Charters and Protocols designed for general acceptance (with a due regard for Africa and Asia). Interpretation of rights mainly derived from the West's Christendom, promotion and public education were the tasks for a world community.

Inevitably, and in brief, over 60 years, the fine, full declaration of 'enduring rights' has been argued over and questioned. Rights that were considered to be economic, social and cultural in their conception and admissibility have been put up against the 'realities' of everyday existence. To what degree can rights be guaranteed? What of the ethnic and religious differences that make common implementation of rights sketchy and contestable? We are determined to ensure fairness and equality for all. How, then, do we deal with evasion, compromise and violation by those self-serving states who are out of line? When international laws forbids outside interference 'in matters essentially within the jurisdiction of member states'? In any case, when such terms as 'terrorist state', 'rogue state' and 'axis of evil' are used do they not thinly veil our inclination to intervene to put things 'right' by putting riddance to terrorists?

There are, fortunately, monitors to watch out for success and failure in rights observance: Amnesty International, Liberty, Human

Rights Watch, the American Civil Liberties Union, the Human Rights Council and the European Court of Human Rights. In Europe, there are other legal watchdogs, Eurojust and the European Judicial Network, an innovative, perhaps experimental framework, although one may wonder just how far the law is able to dissipate the vagaries of instability and fear.

According to UN spokesmen it is chiefly during the last two decades that 'the validity of human rights consensually agreed has been put into sharp focus by the menace of unrelenting terrorist violence'. Terrorism has to be dealt with by anti-terrorism, judicial measures and by counter-terrorism, the physical means of prevention, deterrence, control and stability restoration. States, of course, are keen to represent their responses as ordered, lawful, candid, clear, rational and fair to their people. Unhappily, evidence points to wide and increasingly repressive laws and tactics by governments worried and harried by episodic violence. On occasion they justify their own prerogative of terrorist-like violence, ironically to bring about peace. Examples of this have been witnessed in Northern Ireland, Pakistan, Spain, Iraq, Chechnya, Argentina and Central Africa. The advice of Jack Goldsmith, a security advisor to President Bush, 'Always trust your Government' rings a little hollow.

The record of what is happening in regard to counter-terrorism and rights maintenance, as we have seen, points up a number of debatable issues. How lethal to society are 'direct' and 'indirect' threats of violence? Can we easily tell them apart? What, after all, do we really understand by 'security' and 'safety' and in what ways does a government set out to assure us about them? Are there tolerance limits to what are referred to as militant dissent, terrorist provocation and violent criminal intent beyond which no responsible government can afford to go? Some states detect 'radicals' and 'radicalisations' round every corner. Numerous security procedures in the United States and in the United Kingdom excite queries, unease and vigorous protest, above all, in relation to the isolating and charging of 'suspects', their handling at interview, their detention and possible incarceration in Guantanamo or Belmarsh. Aspects of surveillance, extradition and extraordinary rendition strike us as gross, immoral and, often, illegal. Rights are regarded as jettisoned where there is overmuch personal intervention, discrimination and minority alienation.

Finally, there faces us the question of prevention-via-prediction, something that troubles most counter-terrorism administrators. Around the world there are places where hunger, exploitation and dispossession are endemic, often exacerbated by minority strife. These are the gathering grounds of terrorism. International development schemes do bite into the problems to some extent. These areas are considered to be 'fragile' states or 'weak' states with 'terrorist potential'. Forecasting is notoriously difficult. It is very much a question of where next? And of what next? Understandably, international and regional mega-strategies cannot hoist prevention into place where there will be so much variability in that classic trio of factors pushing a readiness to act violently, namely, motivation-capability-opportunity. How best do we deal with possible scenarios of anguish, those rescuers collectively on the outside and those apprehensive ones on the inside? For the latter, it has been said, 'human rights begin with breakfast', that is, if breakfast arrives. It would be worthwhile to remember Bill Clinton's preparedness to listen and learn a little before we clumsily misjudge the genesis of instability erupting as violence.

The Future? All things to all men, perhaps. A future development in terrorism is the possible use of Weapons of Mass Destruction (WMD). Much expert thought has revolved around the conundrum of the practicability of acquiring weapons of mass destruction, that is, those substances and those methods of collection, assembly, design, emplacement or launching which would then pose a grave threat to large numbers of people. In June 1994 the AUM Shinrikyo fanaticists in Japan were prepared to shower Tokyo with Sarin nerve gas. There are reports that agents of al-Qaida have been scouting suppliers of uranium and initiating discussions with nuclear-bomb trained personnel. It is not impossible that some of the terrorists could infiltrate laboratories and production plants where biological agents are stored for use in herbicides and crop modification. An escalation in lethality is the thing least likely to worry those who contrived the mass horror of 9/11. Given the probable rate of dispersion of a mass weapon, the fallout on a vulnerable, 'soft target', civilian population would be spectacular indeed with possible radiation consequences.

Reconciliation is a carefully approached future outcome of intelligent counter-terrorism. Listening, talking, waiting, risk acceptance, candour and patience are all elements in procedures which move into a fraught conflict situation. Basically, words not weaponry nor strength of arm are the operative tools. Northern Ireland and apartheid-gripped South Africa are examples of political easement leading to disarmament and settlement.

It is a 'leap of faith' on both sides that brings some sort of engagement with a former enemy. Yet, there is anxiety. Does 'their' readiness to confer earn them credibility as representative of a cause? Are we 'giving in' to those we ostracised and attempted to beat? Dare we set out on a path to bring together people who were standing completely apart? In attempting to reconcile diversity in what way can we enrol those latterly isolated in conflict so that they now are accepted as responsible political actors? They dared all this in Belfast, Cape Town and London some years ago and it bore fruit. Cynics will say that this approach is more disengagement than engagement. They will refer to the situation in autumn 2008 when South Africa's Rainbow Nation was being torn, from time to time, by political infighting. Was the gun just laid aside as it was in Antrim, Northern Ireland as former IRA hotheads sent fusillades at the police? Nevertheless, peaceful means of counter-terrorism are being tried and will be tried further.

Another example of attempted reconciliation makes headlines now as well as something encouraging experiment. 'Should we talk with the Taliban?' would have been a heinous suggestion 12 months ago. Gordon Brown, Britain's Prime Minister (according to *The Belfast Telegraph* of 12 March 2007) is ready to open dialogue with Afghanistan's tribal elders, many of them confidants of the Taliban. The chance could be opened up through Afghan Government mediators. Des Browne, Britain's Defence Minister has come out further forward:

what you need to do in conflict resolution is to bring the people who believe that the answer to their political ambition will be achieved through violence into a frame of mind that they accept that their political ambitions will be delivered by politics.

In a similar vein, on 9 October 2008, US Defense Secretary, Robert Gates, told a Budapest NATO meeting who were wearying of war: 'there has to be ultimately – and I'll underscore ultimately – reconciliation as part of a political outcome to this. That's ultimately the exit strategy for all of us'. General David Petraeus, with overall responsibility for US forces in Iraq and Afghanistan, appears to be in broad assent.

The new US President, Barack Obama, on his second day in office, 22 January 2009, set about dismantling the Bush Administration procedures for dealing with terrorism suspects. Guantanamo is to be closed within 12 months. Certain methods of coercive interrogation like torture and 'water-boarding' are prohibited. The new Administration will not now generally rely upon any legal opinion issued by the Bush Justice Department in regard to countering terrorism after 9/11. America's unswerving commitment to the Geneva Convention is renewed. The International Committee of the Red Cross is to keep records of all detainees in

US custody. The network of secret prisons around the world, the CIA 'black sites', that hold an undisclosed number of 'ghost detainees' in Afghanistan, North Africa, South-east Asia and the Balkans, are all to be shut down as soon as possible. The 'rendition' flights transporting suspects to incarceration will be finished with.

Human rights organisations worldwide are likely to greet Obama's dispensation with great relief. Some administration quarters in Washington are showing less enthusiasm about the new deal. Will a number of CIA officials and others be prosecuted for doing what is now judged unlawful? Where are the presumed terrorist detainees to be accommodated on release (especially those in Guantanamo who have never been legally charged or properly tried)?

As we have seen already, the business of asserting and maintaining human rights in our counter-terrorism work is alive with qualification and difficulty.

Two terms, in the future, could well be in the counter-terrorism operative's handbook: 'reconciliation' and 'ultimately'. Patience, though, will be pre-eminent. Philip Heyman of Harvard Law School puts it thus:

As we choose strategies we must see that extremely dangerous terrorism is likely to be around for longer than we can safely suspend democratic freedoms . . . without losing the habits and attitudes democracy depends upon.

In other respects the United States now offers encouraging prospects with change of president. Barack Obama, during the long, 2008 election campaign, declared his position boldly and in some detail on such debatable issues as the Iraq war, nuclear terrorism, counter-terrorism and the human and civil problems it raised, homeland security funding, nuclear weapons dismantlement in North Korea and Libya and the closure of Guantanamo.

It is the last, future possibility that has raised hopes widely but brought in a number of legal difficulties. On closure some time would elapse before new US legal procedures could constitutionally substitute conventional US courts for the camp's military commissions. Conventional procedures, though, would have to address particular security problems such as the reliance on anonymity and the use of secret, classified evidence. Redefinition of 'criminality' would be desirable. Would detainees, however much they were hauled before court, be denied freedom by a further detention regime? What shape might this take? After five years of incarceration without charge would any compensation be payable? Were those released or those on charge to be returned to their country of origin? In 2007 the US Senate had been opposed to this return. And would any form of rehabilitation be possible for those detainees prepared to go through with it? Indeed, the future lines of these seemingly liberal proposals put about by the Obama team are unclear. Should 'We can' be rephrased as 'Ought we?'

Glossary

ACLU   American Civil Liberties Union

AIVD   General Intelligence and Security Service (Netherlands)

Al-Qaida   Osama bin Laden founded this terrorist group in 1989

ASEAN   Association of South-East Asian States

ATCSA   Anti-Terrorism Crime and Security Act 2001 (UK)

AUM Shinrikyo   Japanese terrorist band responsible for 1995 Tokyo attack

CCTV   Closed circuit television for security surveillance

CFSP   Common Foreign and Security Police – Council of Europe (an inter-governmental body, not the European Union), 1997

CIA   Central Intelligence Agency (US)

CODEXTER   Commitee of terrorism experts – Council of Europe (see above)

COREPER   Security monitoring body – Council of Europe (see above)

CTC   Counter-Terrorism Committee – UN Security Council

DHS   Department of Homeland Security (US)

DOJ   Department of Justice (US)

ECHR   European Convention on Human Rights

EJN   European Judicial Network

ETA Euskadi ta Askatasuna – Basque terrorist movement in Spain

EU European Union

FBI Federal Bureau of Investigation (US)

FCO Foreign and Commonwealth Office (UK)

FTOs Foreign Terrorist Organizations – terrorist groups list (US)

IACHR Inter-American Commission on Human Rights (US)

ICJ International Court of Justice

ICRC International Committee of the Red Cross

IRA Irish Republican Army

JTAC MI5's Joint Terrorism Analysis Centre (UK)

JTTF Joint Terrorist Task Force – FBI (US)

MI5 MI5 security agency (UK)

NATO North Atlantic Treaty Organisation

NSA National Security Agency (US)

NSL National Security Letters

OAS Organization of American States

Patriot Act Act for Uniting and Strengthening America by Providing Appropriate Tools required to Intercept and Obstruct Terrorism (US)

PMOI People's Mujahedin of Iran

SIS Schengen Information Service – security database (Europe)

SUS Stop-and-undertake-search procedure

TTIC Terrorist Threat Integration Center – FBI (US)

UN United Nations

US/USA United States of America

WMD Weapons of Mass Destruction

Where to find out more

There are now a good number of books about terrorism and counter-terrorism though not many dealing with human rights and the complex task of countering-terrorists. Readers may find helpful one or two of my own books written especially with the need to bring issues to the fore as clearly as possible.

Whittaker, David J. (2004) *Terrorists and Terrorism in the Contemporary World*. New York: Routledge.

Whittaker, David J. (2007) *Terrorism: Understanding the Global Threat* (2nd edition). Longman.

Whittaker, David J. (2007) *The Terrorism Reader* (3rd edition). London: Routledge.

Informative and plain speaking are two books by the veteran American, Walter Laqueur:

Laqueur, W. (2002) *A History of Terrorism*. Piscataway, NJ: Transaction Publishers.

Laqueur, W. (2003) *No End to War. Terrorism in the 20th Century*. New York: Continuum Press.

More academic treatment by Britain's foremost authorities in St Andrew's University, Scotland, in their Centre for the Study of Terrorism and Political Violence (CSTPV):

Ranstorp, M. and **Wilkinson, P.** (2007) *Terrorism and Human Rights*. Routledge.

Wilkinson, P. (2006) *Terrorism versus Democracy: The Liberal State Response* (2nd edition). Routledge.

The following books have been found very useful:

Apter, D. E. (ed.) (1997) *The Legitimation of Violence*. London: Macmillan.

Ashdown, Lord Paddy 'International Humanitarian Law and Reconciliation in a Changing World' Hauser International Lecture Publish 2004: New York.

Begg, Moazzam (2008) *Enemy Combatant*. Pocket Books.

Bjørgo, Tore (ed.) (2005) *Root Causes of Terrorism: Myths, Reality and Ways Forward*. Abingdon , Oxon: Routledge.

Foot, R. (c2004) *Human Rights and Counter-terrorism in America's Asia Policy*. Oxford: Oxford University Press.

Hayward, K. and **Morrison, W.** (2002) *Cultural Criminology Unleashed*. Routledge.

Heymann, P. B. (2003) *Terrorism, Freedom, and Security: Winning Without War*. Cambridge, MA: MIT Press.

Hoffman, B. (2006) *Inside Terrorism* (2nd rev. edition). New York: Columbia University Press.

Horgan, J. (2005) *The Psychology of Terrorism*. Abingdon, Oxon: Routledge.

Khatchadourian, H. (1998) *The Morality of Terrorism*. New York: Peter Lang.

Marty, D. (2006) The Council of Europe report. Council of Europe, Brussels.

Meltzer, David (2002) *Give War a Chance*. John Hopkins Press.

Pojman, L. P. (2006) *Terrorism, Human Rights, and the Case for World Government*. Lanham, MD: Rowman and Littlefield.

The Council of Europe report by

Many readers will be used to searching and, to some extent, selecting material via the Internet. These sites have proved most productive alongside the use of keywords:

Amazon
www.amazon.co.uk

Amnesty International
www.amnesty.org.uk
www.amnestyusa.org

Centre for Defence and International Security Studies (CDiSS)
www.cdiss.org

European Union
http://europa.eu/index_en.htm

Human Rights Watch USA
www.FrontlineDefenders.org

International Policy Institute of Counter-Terrorism; (Israel)
www.ict.org.il

Liberty
www.yourrights.org.uk

Terrorism Research Center (USA)
www.terrorism.com

United Nations
http://www.un.org/en/index.shtml

US State Department Office of Counter-Terrorism
www.state.gov and www.global.terrorism.index.htm

Index